SIMPLIFYING ACCOUNTING LANGUAGE:
Don't Lose Your Balance!

SIMPLIFYING ACCOUNTING LANGUAGE:

Don't Lose Your Balance!

Jeffrey Slater

North Shore Community College

Cartoons by Gary Woodbury

KENDALL/HUNT PUBLISHING COMPANY

2460 Kerper Boulevard, Dubuque, Iowa 52001

Reviewer
  Donald Litzinger
  Monroe Community College
  Rochester, New York

Printed in the United States of America   C   402010   01

Dedicated to my lovely family
Shelley, Rusty, and Abby

Contents

Preface, **ix**

Acknowledgments, **xi**

Definitions and Illustrations, **1**

Crossword Puzzles and Accounting Hunt, **219**

Solutions to Puzzles and Hunt, **243**

Appendix I—Accounting: Common Formulas and Equations, **247**

Appendix II—Review of Accounting I, II, **253**

Appendix III—Key Managerial and Cost Terms, **263**

Index, **265**

Student Summary Aid

Preface

As a faculty member in an Accounting Department, I constantly heard a consistent criticism from students that accounting textbooks or study guides are not really answering *all* the questions a student may have. My students had great difficulty in simplifying accounting language. I was asked many times to come up with simple definitions, simple examples to back up these definitions, and some type of organization which would get the point across in a clear and understandable manner.

With this student criticism the birth of *Don't Lose Your Balance* took place. The goal of the book is not to replace an accounting textbook, nor the accounting instructor, nor the accounting laboratory assistant. Rather, its intent is to provide a resource which contains many of the basic accounting definitions along with simple supporting material. Once you utilize this book (in class or out) you can then *return* to your text, to your laboratory assistant or to your instructor and build upon the simplicity that has been presented. Making accounting simple is by no means an easy objective. My format of providing students with a simplified approach to understanding accounting has been debated by many people in the field, asking what type of people really could use a book of this nature. In answer to this question the following people could benefit from this supplementary work:

1. A student in an Accounting I or II course.
2. Those in upper accounting courses as a reference to basic accounting theory.
3. A student in Continuing Education and Community Service.
4. People who have had an Accounting I course but who would now like to review before entering Accounting II.
5. People in laboratory settings.
6. Secretaries in offices who would like quick reference.
7. Businessmen (managers and proprietors) as a reference guide.
8. Students in a Basic Bookkeeping course.

The criticisms of students are now being heard and I hope the goal of providing a simple and understandable approach to supplement a basic accounting course will provide you with much satisfaction and reward in your educational advancement—but please, *Don't Lose Your Balance!!*

P.S. Don't forget to try the Accounting Review crossword puzzles at the end of the book:

The crosswords deal with:

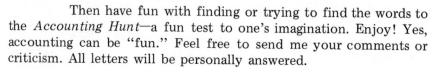

1. Rules of dr., cr., and normal balances
2. Adjusting and closing entries
3. Journals
4. Accruals and deferrals
5. Depreciation
6. Notes and interest
7. Corporations
8. Merchandise company (cost of goods sold)
9. Voucher system
10. Accounting I, II Mix.

Then have fun with finding or trying to find the words to the *Accounting Hunt*—a fun test to one's imagination. Enjoy! Yes, accounting can be "fun." Feel free to send me your comments or criticism. All letters will be personally answered.

Jeffrey Slater

NEW FEATURES OF SECOND EDITION

Based on our class testing and reviewer feedback the second edition has given us the opportunity to clarify, rearrange, and expand many of our terms. We have added 3 new appendixes that illustrate key accounting formulas as well as present a detailed tabloid review of Accounting I and II. The third appendix also introduces key terms from managerial and cost accounting. Take the time on the inside back cover to see our presentation of Key Financial Ratios.

Acknowledgments

In order for me to keep *my* balance, I would like to thank the following people for their comments, criticisms as well as support, in attempting to make a practical student guide to supplement a basic accounting course:

Aristomenes P. Boratgis
Gordon Brown
John G. Butler
Tony Cotoia
Peter R. Doran
Neal Keefe-Feldman
Warren Ford
Joseph P. Francis
John Graham
Paul C. Gullette
James P. Regan
William M. Rowe

I would also like to thank my three hard working secretaries, Laura Moore, Judy Goyette, and Linda Keegan, as well as our accounting lab assistants, Beth Bernstein and Bill Metzner.

Special thanks to John Sullivan, the department chairman, for his continued support throughout.

To Shelley, Rusty, and Abby, "It's nice to be home again."

Definitions and Illustrations

ACCOUNT

A device or place which records and summarizes the increases or decreases of an individual account, ex: cash, accounts payable, sales, rent expense.

(See: balance column account)
T-Account

Date		Description (accounts)	Folio (PR)*	Debit				Credit				Balance			
198X June	4		1		5	0	00						5	0	00
	5		1	1	4	0	00					1	9	0	00
	10		2					1	0	0	00		9	0	00

Account Title   Account #

*PR-Post Reference

$90 is the up to date balance after $100 credit was entered.

ACCOUNTING

A language used to record, summarize, and communicate financial data concerning a person's or company's financial position in an orderly and efficient manner.

Public Accounting	Private Accounting	Government Accounting
Tax consulting	Internal auditing	OMB
Management consultant	Controller	Department
Auditing	Cost accounting	Individual
	Budgeting	agencies

*(See rules of debits and credits.)

3

ACCOUNTING CYCLE

The *complete* process or procedure used in each accounting period that *begins* with the recording (journal entries) of transactions in a business and *ends* with the preparation of a post-closing (post-clearing) trial balance.

The Eight Accounting Commandments

1. *Thou shalt journalize transactions*

   (See journals, journalizing transactions)

2. *Thou shalt post to the ledger accounts*

   (See posting)

3. *Thou shalt prepare a trial balance*

   (See trial balance)

4. *Thou shalt prepare a work sheet*

   (see work sheet)

5. *Thou shalt prepare financial statements*

   (See balance sheet, classified balance sheet, income statement, capital statement)

6. *Thou shalt journalize and post adjusting entries to bring ledger accounts up to date.*

   (See adjusting entries)

7. *Thou shalt journalize and post closing entries.*

   (See temporary accounts, closing entries)

8. *Thou shalt prepare a post-closing trial balance*

   (See post-closing trial balance)

4

ACCOUNTING EQUATION*

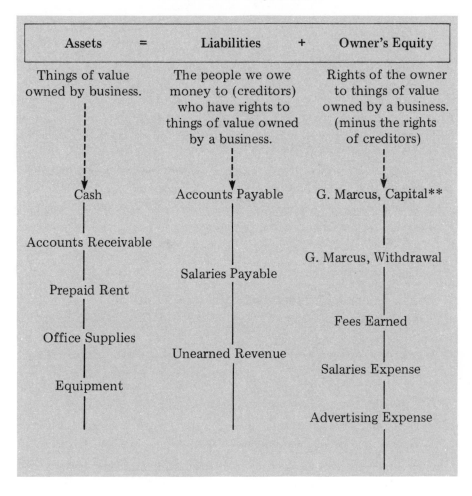

Assets	=	Liabilities	+	Owner's Equity
Things of value owned by business.		The people we owe money to (creditors) who have rights to things of value owned by a business.		Rights of the owner to things of value owned by a business. (minus the rights of creditors)
Cash		Accounts Payable		G. Marcus, Capital**
Accounts Receivable				G. Marcus, Withdrawal
Prepaid Rent		Salaries Payable		
Office Supplies				Fees Earned
Equipment		Unearned Revenue		Salaries Expense
				Advertising Expense

*For a corporation see stockholder's equity.

**As revenue ↑ capital ↑
  As expense ↑ capital ↓

5

ACCOUNTING PERIOD

A regular period of time which is used to identify and relate information about a business during its lifetime.

(See fiscal year or calendar year)

Accounting Period

John went to his accountant to get some information about how long an accounting period is.

John was told by the accountant that the minimum time is usually one month and a possible maximum is one year.

There is no one definite amount of time.* Although 13 four week periods are used to give the best comparisons.

ACCOUNTING PRINCIPLES (CONCEPTS)

Flexible rules established by the accounting profession to help or provide guidelines for a business when it carries out the accounting cycle.

(See principles of . . . for more detail) (As well as accounting cycle)

Accounting Principles

Abbey Ellen decided to open up a sweater company. Her accountant told her that a good accounting system should record, process, summarize, and communicate information in an orderly and efficient manner (to her stockholders, creditors, etc.).

The accountant gave Abbey a book of *accounting principles*, along with the latest newsletters from the accounting board that discussed various *guidelines* or *principles* that Abbey may adopt in carrying out her accounting procedures in preparing her financial reports.

---

*Most companies operate on a 12 month (or one year) accounting period.

ACCOUNTS PAYABLE

Money owed for merchandise or services obtained on account. (Buy now, pay later!) Accounts payable has a credit balance and is found on the balance sheet.

(See accounts receivable)

Accounts Payable

John went to see the Redstockings play baseball at Fenway Park; however, he lost his wallet and had to promise the Redstockings he would pay for his ticket when he found his wallet.

John calls the Redstockings an *accounts payable* because he owes them money. Meanwhile, what do the Redstockings call John . . . Yep, accounts receivable.

ACCOUNTS PAYABLE LEDGER (SUBSIDIARY LEDGER)*

A book or file which contains the records of the *individual people* or companies we owe money to. (This book or file is *not* found in the general ledger.)

If we add up *each* individual customer or company account in the subsidiary ledger that we owe money to, the total of all the individual accounts should equal the *one* figure in the controlling account (accounts payable) in the general ledger after postings.

The sum of the accounts payable ledger (subsidiary ledger) is equal to the *one* figure in the controlling account (accounts payable) in the general ledger after postings.

(See controlling account-accounts payable)

*Is arranged in alphabetical order. 7

ACCOUNTS RECEIVABLE

It is the amount charged or owed to a company by its customers from a sale of merchandise or services on account. Accounts receivable has a debit balance and is found on the balance sheet.

(See accounts payable)

Accounts Receivable

Jill went to see the Redstockings play baseball at Fenway Park; however, she lost her wallet and had to promise the Redstockings she would pay for her ticket when she found her wallet.

The Redstockings call Jill an *accounts receivable* because eventually she will pay them cash. What does Jill call the Redstockings . . . Yep, accounts payable because Jill owes them money.

ACCOUNTS RECEIVABLE LEDGER (SUBSIDIARY LEDGER)*

A book or file which contains the specific or the *individual* records of the amount individual *customers owe us*. (This book or file is *not* found in the general ledger.)

If we add up what *each* customer or company in the subsidiary ledger owes us it should equal the *one* figure in accounts receivable in the general ledger (the controlling account) after postings.

The sum of the accounts receivable ledger (subsidiary ledger) is equal to the *one* figure in the controlling account in the general ledger (accounts receivable) after postings.

(See controlling account—accounts receivable)

*Is arranged in alphabetical order.

ACCRUAL BASIS OF ACCOUNTING

Net income = revenue earned—expenses incurred (that resulted) in earning that revenue

Under this system: (1) A sale is a sale when you *earn it, whether you receive money or not,* contrary to a cash basis system that states that a sale is a sale when you *get* the cash (check). (2) When some expenses are *accumulating or building up,* but *have not been paid* for because they are not yet due, the expenses are recognized and recorded in the year that they occurred even though they will not be paid until next year. This is contrary to a *cash basis system* that says an expense is recognized (or recorded) by a company only when they pay *cash* for it. Under cash basis no consideration is given to whether or not the company is *matching* the true or correct expense with revenue.

(See cash basis of accounting)

Accrual Basis of Accounting

(An example of accrued sales [revenue])

On December 15, 1985 Jim Thorpe (owner of Thorpes' Dog Sitting Service) agreed to walk Mrs. Perron's dog for one month. On January 15, 1986, Mrs. Perron will pay Jim $100.

On December 31, 1985, how much revenue has Jim *really earned* from this job? → 2 weeks X $25 per week = $50.

So Jim makes an adjusting entry:

Journal   Page #1

Date		Description (accounts)	Folio (pr)	Debit	Credit
1985 Dec.	31	Accounts receivable-Perron	2	5 0 00	
		Earned revenue	4		5 0 00

Jim's company has earned $50 of sales (revenue) although he hasn't received the cash yet.

Remember, a *sale is a sale* under the accrual method when it is *earned* whether you receive money or not. (See accrued expenses.)

9

ACCRUED EXPENSES

Expenses that are *accumulating* or *building up* that are not recorded or paid for because payment is not yet due. They really represent an expense in the old year.

(See matching concept)
Reversing entry

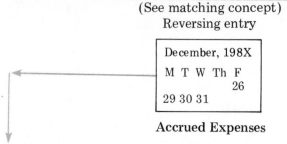

December, 198X

M T W Th F
             26
29 30 31

Accrued Expenses

Jim Jackson owns a restaurant. He pays salaries every two weeks as follows:

cook	$400/per week	($80 per day)
receptionist	$100/per week	($20 per day)
waitresses	$200/per week	($40 per day)
Total salaries =	$700/per week	

On December 26, Jim paid his salaries:

Journal   Page #1

Date		Description (accounts)	Folio (PR)	Debit	Credit
198X Dec.	26	Salary expense	4	7 0 0 00	
		Cash	1		7 0 0 00

On December 31, 197X, Jim wants to *adjust* or *bring up to date* the restaurant's true expenses in the *old year* that resulted in earning those sales in the old year.

He figured he owed salaries as follows for December 29, 30, and 31:

cook	$80 X 3 days	=	$240
receptionist	$20 X 3 days	=	60
waitresses	$40 X 3 days	=	120
			$420

The following adjusting entry was made:

Journal   Page #1

Date	Description (accounts)	Folio (PR)	Debit	Credit
198X Dec. 31	Salary expense	4	4 2 0 00	
	Salary payable	6		4 2 0 00

Jim *will not pay cash for this expense until January* (the next payroll), but it is an expense in the year it resulted in earning revenue in the old year.

Key Point: As the expense is incurred a liability results.

Please Note: This example has shown the use of accrued expenses with adjusting entries. The concept of accruals and amounts could have been shown without reference to adjusting entries.

ACCRUED INTEREST EXPENSE

Interest (cost of using someone else's money) which is *building up* or *accumulating* for which payment is not due, or recorded in our accounting books.

The interest expense is *not* postponed to next year even though we will not pay for it until next year (it is an *expense* in the old year).

(See matching concept for further help)

11

Accrued Interest Expense

Dec. 16 Miro Company needed a loan and went to Glory Bank.

Glory lent $10,000 to Miro at an interest rate of 6% (cost of using the bank's money) for 60 days.

Miro made the following entry:

Journal					Page #1

Date		Description (accounts)	Folio (PR)	Debit	Credit
198X Dec.	16	Cash	1	10000000	
		Notes payable	12		10000000
		(6% 60 days)			

On December 31, Miro wanted to adjust or bring up to date the *true* interest expense in the old year that resulted in allowing Miro Company to use the $10,000 for 15 days (Dec. 16-Dec. 31).

The following adjusting entry was made:

Journal					Page #1

Date		Description (accounts)	Folio (PR)	Debit	Credit
198X Dec.	31	Interest expense*	14	2500	
		Interest payable	13		2500

*6% 60 days $10,000 = 1% of $10,000 or $100 (move decimal two places to the left)

6% 15 days $10,000 = 1/4 of $100 or $25.

(See 6% 60-day method for further help)

12

The company *will not pay* the bank the interest until next year, but the 15 days of *interest is an expense in the year it resulted.*

ACCRUED REVENUE

Revenue that has been *earned* (that are building up or accumulating) but has not been recorded because money has not been received yet.

(See accrual basis of accounting)

Accrued Revenue

On December 15, 1985 Rusty Slater (owner of Slater's Dog Walking Service) agreed to walk Mrs. Jones' dog for one month. On January 15, 1986 Mrs. Jones will pay Rusty $100.

On December 31, 1985 how much sales (revenue) has Rusty really *earned* from this job? ⟶ 2 weeks X $25/per week = $50

So Rusty makes an adjusting entry:

Journal   Page #1

Date		Description (accounts)	Folio (PR)	Debit	Credit
1985 Dec.	31	Accounts receivable	3	5000	
		Revenue earned (accru. rev.)	13		5000

Mrs. Jones owes Rusty $50.

Rusty's company has *earned* $50 although he hasn't received the cash yet.

Key Point: As accrued revenue is collected accounts receivable will decrease and cash will increase. Revenue is *not* recorded *twice.*

ACCUMULATED DEPRECIATION

An account which stores or contains the estimated depreciation *expense* that is taken when spreading the original cost of a piece of equipment or building over a specific period of time.

As the *value* of accumulated depreciation increases, it really reduces what the piece of equipment or building is worth on the business's accounting *books*.

Equipment — accumulated depreciation = worth of equipment on accounting books. The cost amount of this asset indicates the amount that has not yet been depreciated.*

(See depreciation)

Accumulated Depreciation

Joe Francis bought a new car for $5,000.**

At the time of the transaction, the following value of the car appeared on the accounting books:

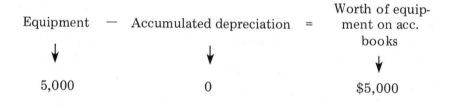

Equipment	—	Accumulated depreciation	=	Worth of equipment on acc. books
↓		↓		↓
5,000		0		$5,000

---

*This is called historical cost. It will not change. It represents the actual cost of the equipment.

**(Assuming that the car will depreciate $1,000 for each of the first four years.)

14

After one year the car has depreciated $1,000.

The car is now worth the following on the accounting books at end of one year:

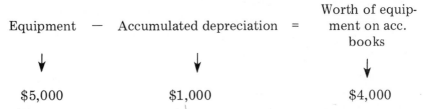

Equipment	—	Accumulated depreciation	=	Worth of equipment on acc. books
↓		↓		↓
$5,000		$1,000		$4,000

After two years the car has depreciated another $1,000.
The car is now worth the following on the accounting books:

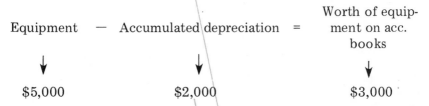

Equipment	—	Accumulated depreciation	=	Worth of equipment on acc. books
↓		↓		↓
$5,000		$2,000		$3,000

(The value of the car on the accounting books doesn't always indicate the real value of the car in the real world). A good example is an antique car which has been fully depreciated but is worth more now than when it was first built.

Depreciation is a *paper entry* which *does not effect cash directly*, but does increase a business's expense, resulting in less profits and, therefore, paying less in taxes which is indirectly a cash savings.

Accumulated depreciation

Dr.	Cr.
	1,000 (year 1)
	1,000 (year 2)
	($2,000 balance)

Key Point: Accumulated depreciation, a contra asset is increased by a credit. Accumulated depreciation is found on the balance sheet.

ADJUSTED TRIAL BALANCE

When the old or original trial balance (list of the ledger) is updated by entries (or what are called adjusting entries) that bring *certain* accounts in the original trial balance up to date, a new or *adjusted trial balance* is formed.

(See work sheet)

Adjusted Trial Balance

Before Adjustments ⟶ After Adjustments

Bill Rowe Real Estate			Bill Rowe Real Estate		
Trial balance Dec. 31, 198X			Adjusted trial balance Dec. 31, 198X		
	Dr.	Cr.		Dr.	Cr.
Cash	1,000		Cash	1,000	
Prepaid rent	400		Prepaid rent*	300	
Office supplies	300		Office supplies*	100	
Automobile	4,000		Automobile	4,000	
Acc. dep.-auto		1,000	Acc. dep.-auto		2,000
Bill Rowe, capital		6,800	Bill Rowe, capital		6,800
Bill Rowe, drawings	500		Bill Rowe, drawings	500	
Rent expense	100		Rent expense*	200	
Salary expense	1,000		Salary expense	1,000	
Light expense	500		Light expense	500	
			Supplies expense*	200	
			Dep. expense*	1,000	
Totals	7,800	7,800	Totals	8,800	8,800

*been adjusted or brought up to date

16

Three Adjustments

1. During the past year, Rowe Real Estate *used* up $100 of its prepaid rent (or we say $100 of prepaid rent expired).

   If one looks at the trial balance, prepaid rent is too high (it should be $300) or is *overstated* by $100. The following adjusting entry is made to bring the prepaid rent account up to date:

Journal   Page #1

Date		Folio (PR)	Description (acc)	Debit	Credit
198X Dec.	31	10	Rent expense	100	
		5	Prepaid rent		100

2. In checking the office supplies in the real estate office it was calculated that $100 worth of supplies was *left on hand (or $200 of supplies used up)*. The following adjusting entry was made: (Adjustments deal with amount used up.)

Journal   Page #1

Date		Folio (PR)	Description (acc)	Debit	Credit
198X Dec.	31	7	Supplies expense	200	
		6	Office supplies		200

3. At the end of the year, depreciation had to be taken on the automobile, ($1,000 per year). When depreciation is taken, it is an *expense* and it also *increases accumulated depreciation.* The following adjusting entry was made:

Journal   Page #1

Date		Folio (PR)	Description (acc)	Debit	Credit
198X Dec.	31	12	Depreciation ex.	1,000	
		4	Acc. dep.-auto		1,000

17

ADJUSTING ENTRIES

Journal entries when posted which bring up to date *certain* balances in the ledger accounts at the *end* of an accounting period to their correct or true balance.

(See adjusted trial balance)

Adjusting Entries

Bill Rowe Real Estate

Trial balance December 31, 198X

Cash	1,000	
Prepaid rent	400	
Office supplies	300	
Automobile	4,000	
Accumulated depreciation		1,000
Bill Rowe, capital		6,800
Bill Rowe, drawings	500	
Rent expense	100	
Salary expense	1,000	
Light expense	500	
Totals	**7,800**	**7,800**

3 adjustments

Three Adjustments

1. During the past year, Rowe Real Estate *used* up $100 of its prepaid rent (or we say $100 of prepaid rent expired).

   If one looks at the trial balance, prepaid rent is too high (it should be $300) or is *overstated* by $100. The following adjusting entry is made to bring the prepaid rent account up to date:

Journal   Page #1

Date		Folio (PR)	Description (acc)	Debit	Credit
198X Dec.	31	10	Rent expense	100	
		5	Prepaid rent		100

18

2. In checking the office supplies in the real estate office, it was calculated that $100 worth of supplies was left on hand (or $200 of supplies was used). The following adjusting entry was made:

Journal   Page #1

Date		Folio (PR)	Description (acc)	Debit	Credit
198X Dec.	31	7	Supplies expense	200	
		6	Office supplies		200

3. At the end of the year, depreciation had to be taken on the automobile, ($1,000 per year). When depreciation is taken, it is an expense and it also increases accumulated depreciation. The following adjusting entry was made:

Journal   Page #1

Date		Folio (PR)	Description (acc)	Debit	Credit
198X Dec.	31	12	Depr. expense	1,000	
		4	Acc. dep.-auto		1,000

The result is to then make an adjusted or up to date trial balance.

(See adjusted trial balance to see what *new* trial balance looks like)

Key Point: Adjusting entries when journalized and posted allow the financial reports to reflect up to date balances.

AGING ACCOUNTS RECEIVABLE

A list of *unpaid customers* accounts which show when their bills are due or how many days their bills are overdue.

We can use this list to estimate how many accounts will turn into bad debts (not paying their bills).

(See bad debts for more detail) (See also
schedule of accounts receivable)

Aging Accounts Receivable

List or Schedule of Accounts Receivable by Age
(when Customers' Bills are Due or Past Due)

Customers Name	Not Yet Due	1-30 Days Past Due	31-60 Days Past Due	61-90 Days Past Due	90 Days Past Due
Boratgis	$50				
Reagan	$60				
Rowe		$25			
Sullivan			$100		
Woodbury				$50	
Keegan					$100
Bernstein					$400

We are concerned that *Sullivan, Woodbury, Keegan, and Bernstein* may never pay their bills. Since the selling terms to these customers were 2/10, N/30 (customers could get a 2% discount if they paid their bills within 10 days of the full amount or the bill was due within 30 days).

It is now later than 30 days for Sullivan, Woodbury, Keegan, and Bernstein. *Our greatest concern is with Keegan and Bernstein.*

ALLOWANCE METHOD FOR BAD DEBTS

A method which estimates the amount of bad debts that will result from charge sales during a period of time (how many people will never pay their bills). The estimates may be based on a % of sales or as a % of accounts receivable.

This method matches bad debt expenses to the period of time when the sales were *earned* or recognized.

(See direct write-off method)

(See contra account-accumulated depreciation, allowance for doubtful accounts)

Allowance Method for Bad Debts

During last year, Rudy Ricardy Pants, Inc. had charge sales of $10,000, of which $500 or 5% of the charge sales were expected to become bad debts—(customers who did not pay their bills). This 5% figure was based on the past collection records of the company.

To record this estimated amount of bad debts, the following entry was made at the end of that year:

(Adjusting entry)

Journal   Page #1

Date		Folio (PR)	Description (acc)	Debit	Credit
198X Dec.	31	12	Bad debt expense*	500	
		5	All. for dbtf. ac.		500

(Adjusting entry continues on following page) ─────────

Key Point: The allowance for doubtful account has a credit balance and is a reduction in accounts receivable. This allows receivables to be valued as collectible on the balance sheet.

---

*Also called uncollectable account expense.

(This entry records the bad debt expense in the same year that sales were earned or recognized.) We don't know which customers will turn out to be bad debts.

In the next year, Peter Doran (who had bought some pants *last year*) became a bad debt. The following was recorded to show the bad debt.

Journal   Page #1

Date		Folio (PR)	Description (acc)	Debit	Credit
198X Jan.	15	5	All. for dbtf. ac.	XXX	
		3	A/R—Peter D.		XXX

The debit to the allowance account reduces the reserve for bad debts while the credit to accounts receivable reduces what Peter Doran owes, since it has been assumed he will *never* pay it.

(See direct method for comparison)

Key Point: This accounting procedure utilizing the allowance method tries to match credit sales on account to the estimated amount of bad debts expense. It is the allowance for doubtful accounts that contains this estimate of bad debts.

22

AMORTIZATION

The spreading out (or allocating) the cost of an intangible asset (or bond discount or premium) over the life of the asset (or bond).

Amortization

Paul Gullette Inc. acquired a patent (an exclusive right) to manufacture and sell a new type of camera.

The cost of the patent was $200,000 (that was recorded as a debit to patents and a credit to cash).

At the end of the first year, the following adjusting entry was made: (Paul Gullette Inc. plans to spread the cost of the patent over a 5 year period at $40,000 per year).

Journal   Page #1

Date		Description (accounts)	Folio (PR)	Debit	Credit
198X Dec.	31	Amortization	10	40,000	
		Patents	5		40,000

This entry will be made at the end of each year until the cost of the patent has been spread (or amortized).

(This same type of entry could be used for goodwill, or organization costs, etc.)

Key Point: As the expense is shown, the asset on the balance sheet decreases.

APPROPRIATION OF RETAINED EARNINGS

A portion or part of retained earnings that is *restricted or set aside* for a certain purpose thus making it unavailable for dividend declarations.

Appropriation of Retained Earnings

Stockholders Equity	
Common Stock, $2 par, 5,000 shares	$10,000

Retained earnings:
  Appropriated retained earnings:
    *For plant expansion $5,000
    For payment of bond debts 2,000
    For working capital 1,000	

Total appr. retained earnings $8,000	
Unappropriated retained earnings 1,000	
Total retained earnings	9,000
Total paid-in capital (contributed) and rtd. earnings	$19,000

The journal entry for plant expansion would be:

Journal   Page #1

Date		Description (accounts)	Folio (PR)	Debit	Credit
198X Dec.	10	Retained earnings	14	5,000	
		Retained earnings appropriated for plant expansion	10		5,000

Key Point: Remember retained earnings results from the profit (earnings) that remains in the company.

ASSETS

Things (or properties) of value which make up and are owned by a business. It is the liabilities and capital which show who supplied the assets to the firm.

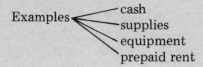

Examples — cash
supplies
equipment
prepaid rent

(See classified balance sheet)

Assets

The assets of Ted Villiams revealed the following:

10 dollars _____ (cash)

1 uniform _____ (supplies)

2 automobiles _____ (equipment)

3 months rent paid in advance for_____ (prepaid rent)
   the use of the Boston Garden

AUDITING

A procedure to determine if the financial reports of a firm are prepared according to general accounting principles and thus reflect reliable and accurate information.

Goals of auditing:
1. Promote efficiency
2. Safeguard assets
3. Reliable information
4. Public confidence
5. System of checks and balances

BAD DEBTS

An expense (or loss) that results when a customer does not pay for some goods or services that were charged to his account.

(See allowance method and/or direct method)

Bad Debts

Edward Newburgh, a foreign student visiting America, was able to charge (buy now, pay later) a television set at Flaires Department Store.

Ed received a letter from his parents asking him to come home immediately.

Ed left America and when he received his bill from Flaires he just *threw it away* (saying he would never return to America).

After many attempts, Flaires decided it wasn't worth the additional cost of trying to *track* Ed down and came to the realization that Ed's bill was a bad debt.

BALANCE COLUMN ACCOUNT

A column in a ledger account which shows a running balance between the debits and the credits. This column summarizes or gives an *up-to-date balance* at the time each entry is recorded.

(See account)

Balance Column Account

Accounts payable (511)

Date		Item	Folio (PR)	Debits	Credits	Balance Debits	Balance Credits
198X Jan.	5		PJ 1*		100		100
	15		CP 2**	50			50

*PJ 1—Purchases Journal Page 1
**CP 2—Cash Payments (cash disbursements) Journal Page 2

On January 15, we owe creditors $50.

BALANCE SHEET (POSITION STATEMENT)

A report or statement which lists or shows the financial position of a business is doing as of a particular date. It gives a history of what is *owned* by the business (assets) and what portion of those assets are *owed* by the business (liabilities) and the owner's claim to the assets of the business (owner equity or capital). Think of assets as the resources of the business.

Assets = liabilities + capital (owner equity)*

(See classified balance sheet for a more detailed type balance sheet).

Balance Sheet

The Redstockings**
Balance Sheet
September 9, 198X

Assets		Liabilities	
Cash	$ 10.00	Accounts payable	$ 50.00
Uniform	50.00	Owner Equity	
Automobile	100.00		
Prepaid rent	50.00	(capital)	
		Ted Villian	160.00
Total assets	$210.00	Total liabilities and owner equity	$210.00

The creditor(s) (accounts payable) that the Redstockings owe money to, has the rights to $50 worth of assets owned by the business until the creditor(s) is paid off by the Redstockings.

Meanwhile, Ted Villian has rights to $160 worth of assets owned by the business.

*For a corporation see stockholders' equity.
**Notice the heading answers the questions: who, what, and when.

BALANCING AND RULING

A way in which the accounts in the ledger are *cleaned up* or summarized after closing entries have been posted to get ready, as well as, to show that one accounting period is over and a new one is about to begin. All temporary accounts will have no balance brought forward.

Balance and Ruling

Account: Office Equipment   Account No. 116

Date		Item	PR	Dr		Date		Item	PR	Cr	
19XX Jul.	18	40	GJ1	100	00	19XX Jul.	31	Adjustment	GJ2	60	00
							31	Balancing	√	40	00
										100	*00*
				100	00					100	00
Aug.	1	Balance Brought Forward	√	40	00						

To start the next accounting period office equipment has a 40 balance.

BANK DISCOUNT

The bank does not give the borrower the *full amount* of the loan because it has deducted the interest (cost of using the bank's money) *ahead of time* instead of waiting until the loan has been paid back and then getting the interest.

Bank Discount

Jill went to the new Sun Bank to borrow $100,000.

The bank agreed to loan Jill the money (at an interest rate of 6%) with the stipulation that the bank would *discount* the loan.

This meant that Jill received $94,000 instead of $100,000. (6% X $100,000 = $6,000 interest taken by the bank before giving the loan to Jill.)

At maturity, or when the loan came due, Jill paid Sun Bank $100,000.

BANK LOAN

The bank gives the borrower the *full amount** of the loan and collects interest (cost or using the bank's money) when the loan is paid back by the borrower.

Bank Loan

Art Calnen went to the new Sun Bank to borrow $100,000.

The bank agreed to loan Art the money at an interest of 6%. (Cost of using the bank's money.)

Art left the bank with $100,000.

At maturity or when the loan came due, Art paid the bank $106,000.

$100,000	Loan
+ 6,000	(6% X $100,000)
$106,000	Paid back to bank at maturity

*Keep in mind any loan from a bank is a bank loan even if a note has been discounted.

BANK RECONCILIATION

A procedure to explain the difference between the bank balance on the bank statement versus the balance of cash in the ledger (checkbook).

(See outstanding checks)

Bank Reconciliation

This is usually found on the back side of a bank reconciliation.

This bank statement showed a bank balance of $425 but the bank had not processed (or cleared) $300 of deposits we made as well as $140 of checks we've written had not been processed by the bank. So actually the true balance is $585.

On the front side of a bank statement the following information could be found:

1. Last months statement balance
2. Number of deposits made this month
3. Service charges (if any)
4. Ending balance on statement
5. List of all checks and deposits that were cleared (or processed by the bank)
6. Some types of bank statements will contain savings account balances.

Checkbook	Bank
—Service charge*	+to deposit intransit
—NSF (bounced checks)	—checks outstanding

*Any changes to checkbook will require journal entries to bring cash and other ledger accounts up to date.

Lion County
Bank

117 Sadle Road** Lynn, Massachusetts   Telephone—745-1174

This form is provided to help you balance your bank statement

Please notify us of any change in address

Checks outstanding
not charged to account

Sort the checks numerically or by
date issued.

check number	amount	
10	$ 15	00
12	100	00
17	25	00
Total	$140	00

Check off on the stubs of your checkbook each of the checks paid by the bank and make a list of the numbers and amounts of those still outstanding in the space provide dat the left.

Also verify the deposits in your checkbook with deposits credited on this statement.

Bank balance shown on this statement	$	4	2	5	0	0
Add deposits not credited on this statement		3	0	0	0	0
Subtotal		7	2	5	0	0
Subtract checks outstanding		1	4	0	0	0
Balance: this should be your correct checkbook balance		5	8	5	0	0

If your checkbook does
. not agree, enter below
any necessary adjustment:

Checkbook balance $

Subtract service charge
(if any) not entered in
checkbook checks
paid, but not entered
in checkbook

**If no errors are reported to
   auditor in ten days the account
   will be considered correct

Subtotal _____

Add $ _____ $ _____

Correct checkbook balance

BEGINNING INVENTORY—MERCHANDISE COMPANY

The amount of goods (merchandise) on hand in a company at the beginning of an accounting period. It is an asset.

The ending inventory at the *end* of an accounting period becomes the *beginning* inventory to start the *next* accounting period.

(See cost of goods sold)

Beginning Inventory—Merchandising Company

This figure for beginning inventory ($19,700) shows the cost to this supermarket for the goods (merchandise on the shelves or in the back room) that it could sell to its customers during the new accounting period before considering additional purchases.

Timothy J. Whelan Supermarket
Income Statement
For year ended December 31, 198X

Revenue from sales:

Sales			$267,736
Less: Sales returns and allowance . .	$ 2,140		
Sales discount	1,822	3,962	
Net sales			$263,774

Cost of merchandise sold:*

Beg. mdse. inventory, Jan. 1, 198X**		$ 19,700	
Purchases	$205,280		
Less purchases discount.	1,525		
Net purchases		203,755	
Merchandise avble. for sale . . .		$223,455	
Less ending mdse. inv. Dec. 31, 198X***		22,150	
Cost of merchandise sold . . .			201,305

Gross profit on sales . . . . $ 62,469

*or cost of goods sold.

**assumed to be sold and thus a cost.

***assumed not to be sold and thus becomes the beginning inventory to start the next accounting period.

BETTERMENT

The process of improving (replacing or repairing) assets in a business. Usually at a cost much greater than existing asset. A betterment may make an asset more productive but not necessarily provide a longer life.

Key Point: Cost of new motor is debited to machinery and cost and any depreciation is removed from the accounts.

BOND

An interest-bearing note payable that the borrower issues to lenders. The bond indenture (written agreement) identifies the specifics of the bond provisions.

(See maker for more detail)

Bond

Vernitrone Corporation was deciding whether to issue more stock or sell *bonds* in an attempt to raise more money for plant expansion.

The one thing the management or Vernitrone carefully analyzed was whether the company, if they chose bonds, could pay back the bonds when they reached their maturity date, as well as pay yearly interest on the bonds over the years.

BOND DISCOUNT

The amount that results when selling bonds to investors when the *market rate* (effective) is *greater than* the *bond rate* (contractual). The account bond discount is a debit balance found in the long term liability section of the balance sheet.

Bond Discount = face value of bond (amount due at maturity before considering interest, payments, etc.) — amount of money investor paid to buy the bonds from a company.

(See bond premium)

Bond Discount

In an attempt to raise money, Marvel Corporation (after going through the proper channels) offered a bond issue of $200,000 at an interest rate (contractual) of 3% annually for 20 years.

This means in 20 years Marvel will pay back:

1. The $200,000 (face amount of the loan) and
2. The interest ($6,000 per year for 20 years or totally $120,000) or the cost of using someone else's money.

When the bonds finally came out to investors, the going market rate for *similar bonds* was a 3 1/2% (effective rate)

Since Marvel bonds paid *less* interest than other bonds of this type, they had to settle for $175,000 (highest bid made by investors). The following entry was made to show the sale of Marvel's bonds:

		Journal		Page #1	
Date		Description (accounts)	Folio (PR)	Debit	Credit
198X Jan.	5	Cash	1	175,000	
		Discount on bonds	8	25,000	
		Bonds payable	10		200,000

(See bond premium for comparison)

Key Point: Selling price is below the face value.

34

BOND—FACE VALUE

The amount of a bond that is to be paid at maturity (when it comes due) *before* considering interest expense, etc., which may have to be paid (or has already been paid).

Bond—Face Value

Boratgis Inc., issued $100,000 worth of 6% 20 year bonds to raise money for plant expansion.

Each year Boratgis Inc. Paid $6,000 interest for the use of this money (6% X $100,000 = $6,000 per year).

When the bonds finally came due, Boratgis Inc. paid back the $100,000 (of the *face value** of the bonds) to the investors.

*The amount stated on the face of the bond.

BOND PREMIUM

The amount that results when selling bonds to investors when the *market rate* (effective) is *less* than the bond rate (contractual). The account bond premium is a credit balance found in the long term liability section of the balance sheet.

Bond Premium = amount of money investors paid to buy bonds from a company — face value (amount due at maturity before considering interest, payments, etc.)

(See bond discount)

Bond Premium

In an attempt to raise money Jones Corporation (after going through the proper channels) offered a bond issue of $200,000 at an interest rate (contractual) of 3% annually for 20 years.

This meant that in 20 years Jones will pay back:
1. The $200,000 (face amount of loan)
2. The interest ($6,000 per year for 20 years or totally $120,000) or cost of using someone else's money.

When the bonds finally came out to investors the going market rate for similar bonds was 2 1/2% (effective rate).

Since Jones' bonds paid more than other bonds of its type, the company received a bid of $225,000 by investors for their bonds (or $25,000 more than they had originally expected). The following entry was recorded to show the sale:

Journal   Page #1

Date		Description (accounts)	Folio (PR)	Debit	Credit
198X Jan.	5	Cash	1	225,000	
		Bonds payable	10		200,000
		Premium on Bonds	9		25,000

(See bond discount for comparison)

Key Point: Selling price is higher than face value.

36

BOOK VALUE—EQUIPMENT

Equipment minus accumulated depreciation equals what equipment is worth on *accounting books* (*book* value).

The equipment may be worth more than *book value* in the real world (when it is traded in, etc.).

(See accumulated depreciation)

Book Value—Equipment

Beth Bernstein, Inc. bought a new truck for $5,000.

Truck (11)		Accumulated dep.—truck	
5,000			0

At the end of the first year, depreciation of $1,000 was taken on the truck by an adjusting entry:

Journal   Page #1

Date		Description (accounts)	Folio (PR)	Debit	Credit
198X Dec.	31	Depreciation expense	12	1,000	
		Accumulated depreciation	5		1,000

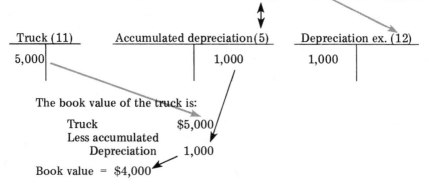

Truck (11)		Accumulated depreciation (5)		Depreciation ex. (12)	
5,000			1,000	1,000	

The book value of the truck is:

Truck	$5,000
Less accumulated Depreciation	1,000
Book value =	$4,000

Key Point: Book value represents the net figure in the reporting of assets on the balance sheet.

37

BOOK VALUE—EQUITY PER SHARE OF STOCK

An estimated value of the claims of a single share of stock in a corporation against the assets of a corporation.

The figure obtained can be very deceptive in that the figure represents an amount that would be given to each stockholders share of stock if a corporation liquidates and doesn't have any expenses, losses, or gains in selling its assets and paying off all the creditors.

(See liquidation/or realization)

Book Value—Equity Per Share of Stock

Fletchers
Stockholders Equity

Preferred 8% stock cumulative, $100 par (100 shares)	$10,000
Premium on preferred stock	2,000
Common stock $5 par (10,000 shares)	50,000
Premium on common stock	5,000
Retained earnings	25,300
Total Equity	$92,300

Fletcher Corporation is liquidating (going out of business) and has a total equity of $92,300 to divide up (find equity per share) between preferred and common stock.

Fletcher, after considering the rights of preferred stockholders (see cummulative and participating), states that each share of preferred stock is entitled to $104 per share or totally $10,400 (100 shares X $104 = $10,400).

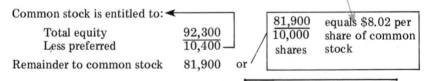

Common stock is entitled to:

Total equity	92,300
Less preferred	10,400
Remainder to common stock	81,900

or

$\dfrac{81,900}{10,000 \text{ shares}}$ equals $8.02 per share of common stock

BOOKKEEPING

The taking of data and recording them in specially designed form (bookkeeping is only one part of a much larger operation called accounting) as set up by accounting principles.

(See accounting principles)

ACCOUNTING

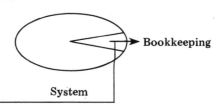

One part of the accounting system which helps to record, process, summarize, and communicate information in an orderly and efficient manner.

BUSINESS ENTITY

A business is separate and distinct from its owners. A corporation is like an artificial person in the eyes of the law.

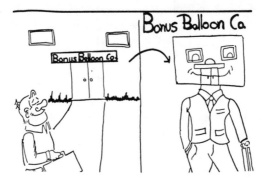

All entities are units requiring the functions of accounting to be performed.

CALENDAR YEAR

A period of time beginning on January 1 and ending December 31 of the same year. All payroll is based on a calendar year.

(For comparison see fiscal year)

CALLABLE BONDS

A type of bond which allows the company to redeem (or take back) for *proper payment* the bond before it reaches its maturity date.

Callable Bonds

On November 1, 197X J.P. Slide Company issued $20,000 worth of callable bonds to investors. These bonds would reach maturity (or come due) in 199X.

However, since these are callable bonds, on January 8, 198X, J.P. Slide notified the holders of the bonds that the company intended to call back in the bonds (for proper payment) before the maturity date. Why did J.P. Slide do it? **?**

Interest rates were falling and they felt it would be cheaper to recall the old bonds and issue new bonds at a lesser interest rate.

CAPITAL (OWNERS' EQUITY) (NET WORTH)

Rights of the owner to things (assets or properties) owned by a business. If you take assets minus liabilities you come up with the rights of the owner.

(For a corporation see stockholders' equity)

Assets
— Liabilities
= Capital

CAPITAL EXPENDITURE
(BALANCE SHEET EXPENDITURES)

After a business buys a plant asset (building) certain expenditures (costs) will result in order to keep the plant asset (building) at its *"full usefulness"* as determined by the business.

If the expenditure (cost) keeps the plant asset at its "full usefulness" for *more than* one accounting period this is called a *capital expenditure.* The capital expenditure increases net assets.

(See revenue expenditure)

This is a major improvement to Walter High School.

CAPITAL STATEMENT

A statement which shows how the value of the owners' rights to assets in a business have changed from one period of time to another. You take his beginning rights, add to it the companies profit, and subtract his withdrawals: the result being a new figure for his rights or new capital (or owner equity) in the business.

Capital Statement

Sullivan Taxi Capital Statement For month ended September 30, 198X		
Beginning capital Sept. 1, 198X		$600,000
Net income for the month	$50,000	
Less withdrawals	(20,000)	
Increase in capital		30,000
New capital Sept. 31, 198X		$630,000

Key Point: Remember revenues and expenses go on an income statement and withdrawals are not business expenses and are thus not placed on the income statement.

CASH BASIS OF ACCOUNTING

(Usually for small company where inventories are not a factor.)

Net income = revenue — expenses

(cash taken in) — (cash going out)

Here we consider:

1. *A sale when we receive money.* This is different from an accrual basis that assumes a sale is a sale when you earn it (whether you receive money or not) and,

2. *An expense when we pay cash* for something versus an accrual system that matches expenses with earned revenues. Under an accrual system an expense is considered an expense, even if money is not paid if it occurs in making sales in that period of time.

Cash Basis of Accounting

Revenue	$160,000*
(Received)	
Expenses	20,000**
Net Income	$120,000

*Earned $200,000, on $160,000 collected in cash.
**Expense of $38,000 incurred only $20,000 paid in cash.

CASH DISCOUNT

A savings off the regular price of goods or services due to early payment of a bill by a customer.

If terms of sale were 2/15, n/60 this means:

If you pay your bill within 15 days of the invoice date, (billing date) you can deduct 2% off the bill; if not, pay the full amount of the bill within 60 days from the date of the invoice.

(See invoice for clarification)

Cash Discount

John got a bill for $100 in the mail with terms of 2/10, n/60.

He showed the bill to his wife who said, "John, *pay the bill within 10 days* and we can take $2* off our bill; but, if we can't pay the bill within 10 days, make sure you pay the full amount of the bill within 60 days."

*2% X $100 = $2.00.

44

CASH DIVIDEND

The amount of cash that a corporation divides or gives out to the stockholders of the corporation, from its earning.

Usually before declaring (or definitely being announced by the corporation that a dividend will be paid) a cash dividend the following is considered:

1. Enough cash.
2. Amount of retained earnings which could be used for dividends.

The amount of retained earnings never shows *how much cash the business has* available to pay out in dividends.

(See: Retained earnings for more detail)
(See: Date of record for more detail)
(See: Date of declaration for more detail)
(See: Date of payment for more detail)

Cash Dividend

On May 8, 198X, the board of directors of Howard Slater Inc. *declared* a 50 cent dividend per share on the 50,000 shares of common stock ($10 par) that had been issued. The following entry was made.*

Journal   Page #1

Date		Description (accounts)	Folio (PR)	Debit	Credit
198X May	8	Retained earnings	10	25,000	
		Cash dividend payable	15		25,000

On June 5, the dividend was paid: the entry was recorded as follows:

Journal   Page #2

Date		Description (accounts)	Folio (PR)	Debit	Credit
198X June	5	Cash dividend payable	15	25,000	
		Cash	1		25,000

*50,000 shares X 50 cents = $25,000

45

CASH DISBURSEMENT JOURNAL
(CASH PAYMENTS JOURNAL)

A book or place (journal) which shows the *outflow or spending of cash* (check) in recording business transactions.

(See special journal)

Cash Disbursements Journal
(Cash Payments Journal)

198X

September

5 Paid Jim Supply Co. what we owed him ($600 less a 20% discount, or $480)

6 Paid Pete's Wholesale Co. $200 we owed them (No discount)

7 Paid $200 for freight to ship some goods

Cash Disbursements Journal

Date	Ck. No.	Accounts Debited	Folio (PR)	Sundry Acct. Debited	Accounts Payable Debited	Purchases Discount Credited	Cash Credit
198X Sept. 5	2	Jim's Supply Co.	✓		600	120	480
6	3	Pete's Whsl. Co.	✓		200		200
7	4	Freight	215	200			200
30		Total		(200)	800	120	880
				(✓)	(250)	(512)	(110)

Posting Rules

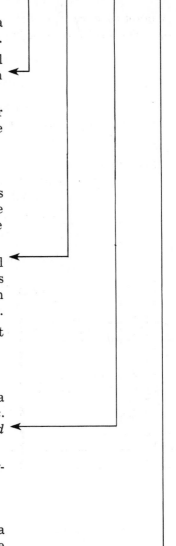

(√)   (250)   (512)   (110)

Sundry

Total of $200 is not posted!! Place a check (√) to show *not* to post total.

The freight is posted to the general ledger at any time during the month as a debit.

When this is done the account number (215) is put into the post reference column.

Accounts Payable

The total ($800) of the column is posted as a debit to accounts payable (acc. #250) in the general ledger at the *end of the month.*

During the month each individual entry (to Jim's supply and Pete's Whsle.) is posted as a debit to each account in the A/P subsidiary ledger.

When this is done, a check (√) is put in the post reference column.

Purchases Discount

Total of column $120 is posted as a credit to purchases discount (acc. #512) in the general ledger at the *end of the month.*

No individual entries are posted during the month.

Cash

Total of column $880 is posted as a credit to cash (acc. #110) in the general ledger *at end of month.*

No individual entries are posted during the month.

CASH RECEIPTS JOURNALS

A book or place (journal) where transactions are recorded when *money* (check) is received from *any* source. (From a sale, note to a bank, etc.)

Cash Receipts Journal

198X

December 1 Jim Smith paid what he owed us ($100, less a 2% discount, or $98).

2 Made a sale to Paul Silas for cash of $200.

4 Borrowed $2,000 cash from a bank.

Cash Receipts Journal

Date	Accounts Name	Folio (PR)	Sundry Account Credit	Sales Credit	Accounts Receivable Credit	Sales Disct. Debited	Cash Debited
198X Dec. 1	Jim Smith	√			100	2.00	98
2	Paul Silas	√		200			200
4	Notes payable	432	2,000				2,000
	Totals		2,000	200	100	2.00	2,298
			(√)	(25)	(220)	(112)	(110)

Posting Rules

Sundry

Total of $2,000 is not posted!! Place a check (√) to show *not* to post total.

Notes payable is posted to general ledger at any time during the month. When this is done the acc. #432 is put into the folio column.

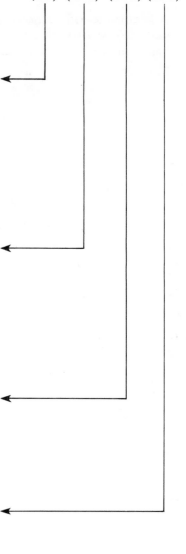

(25) (220) (112) (110)

Sales

Total of column ($200) is posted to sales (acc. #25) as a cr. in the general ledger at the *end of the month.* No individual entries are posted during the month. A check is put in the folio column to show not to post each amount.

Accounts Receivable

The total of the column ($100) is posted as a credit to a/r in general ledger (acc. #220) at *end of month.*

During the month each individual entry (Jim Smith, etc.) is posted *daily* as a credit to the account, in the a/r subsidiary ledger. When this is done a check ($\sqrt{}$) is put in the folio column to show that the posting has been done.

Sales Discount

Total of column ($2.00) is posted as a debit to sales discount in the general ledger (acc. #112) at *the end of the month.* No individual entries are posted during the month.

Cash

Total of column ($2,298) is posted as a debit to cash (acc. #110) in the general ledger at the *end of the month.* No individual entries are posted during the month.

CASH—FLOW STATEMENT

A statement which shows from what source (or where) the cash has *come into* the business, as well as where (or for what) cash has been *spent* by the business.

The result is an increase or decrease in the balance of cash account as of a certain period of time.

(See funds flow)

Cash—Flow Statement

<table>
<tr><td colspan="3" align="center">The Blue Bonnet Lounge
Cash—Flow Statement
For Month of February 198X</td></tr>
<tr><td>*Cash receipts* (money coming in)</td><td>$ 500</td><td></td></tr>
<tr><td>From January sales of liquors
(From customers who are now paying
bills they owed in January)</td><td></td><td></td></tr>
<tr><td>From *cash sales* of liquor duirng Feb.</td><td>1,000</td><td></td></tr>
<tr><td>Total cash coming into business during
month of February</td><td></td><td>$1,500</td></tr>
<tr><td>*Cash payments*</td><td></td><td></td></tr>
<tr><td>Waitresses
Supplies
Inventory of liquor
Rent</td><td>$ 150
100
1,000
100</td><td></td></tr>
<tr><td>Total cash paid out business during
month of February</td><td></td><td>1,350</td></tr>
<tr><td>Increase in cash account</td><td></td><td>$ 150</td></tr>
</table>

CERTIFIED PUBLIC ACCOUNTANT (CPA)

A person who has passed all parts of a state exam qualifying him for a license to practice accounting.

(See each states requirement for more detail)

Practices Public Acct.
Audit Reports
Independent Opinions
Management Consulting

CHART OF ACCOUNTS

A system which shows a classified listing of the names and numbers of account titles being used by an individual business.

Chart of Accounts

Account Title	Account Numbers
Assets:	
Cash	1
Accounts receivable	2
Land	15
Building	21
Office equipment	29
Liabilities:	
Accounts payable	30
Owner equity:	
Abe Sullivan capital	41
Abe Sullivan, withdrawal . .	42
Revenue	
Legal fee	50
Expenses	
Heat	60
Wages	62

CHECK REGISTER

When a company uses a voucher system the check register takes the place of the cash payments (disbursements) journal.

When a voucher is paid from the check register, the result is to reduce vouchers payable (or what we owe from a bill or obligation) and reduce our cash (write a check).

(See voucher register)

Check Register

Date		Payee (who is receiving money)	Voucher Number	Check Number	Debit Voucher Payable Credit Cash
198X Mar.	10	Katz Realty	3	911	300
	12	Russell Sales	5	912	350
	15	J.P. Stationery	8	913	200

(See voucher register for comparison)

March 10 — Paid Katz Realty $300
12 — Paid Russell Sales $350
15 — Paid J.P. Stationery $200

CLASSIFIED BALANCE SHEET (POSITION STATEMENT)

A balance sheet which breaks down assets and liabilities into specific headings or categories (a more detailed balance sheet).

Assets = current assets + plant assets

Liabilities = current liabilities + long-term liabilities

(See: balance sheet for purpose of a balance sheet, long-term investments for another category of assets)

Classified Balance Sheet

Art's Discount Store
Balance Sheet, December 31, 198X

Assets

Current assets:

Cash	$1,000	
Notes receivable	500	
Accounts receivable	400	
Merchandise inventory	2,000	
Prepaid insurance	500	
Office supplies	400	
Store supplies	300	
Total current assets		$5,100

Plant and equipment:

Office equipment	$2,000		
Less accumulated depreciation	1,500	$ 500	
Store equipment	3,000		
Less accumulated depreciation	500	2,500	
Building	2,000		
Less accumulated depreciation	500	1,500	
Land		8,600	13,100
Total plant and equipment			$18,200
Total assets			

Liabilities

Current liabilities: (short-term)

Notes payable	$ 700	
Accounts payable	2,500	
Wages payable	4,000	
Total current liabilities		$7,200

Long-term liabilities:

First mortgage payable, backed by a mortgage on land and blds	5,000	
Total liabilities		$12,200

Owner Equity (capital)

Art Irzyk, capital, January 1, 198X	$5,000	
Net income for the year ended December 31, 198X	$3,000	
Less withdrawals for personal expenses	(2,000)	
Excess of income over withdrawals	1,000	
Art Irzyk, capital, December 31, 198X		6,000
Total liabilities and owner equity		$18,200

COMMON—SIZE STATEMENTS

Statements or reports of companies that just show percentages and do not need to use dollar amounts.

(See vertical and horizontal analysis)

Common-Size Statement

Jerves Company Common Size Income Statement For Year Ended December 31, 198X		
	Sales	100%
(Less)	Cost of goods sold	− 20%
(Equals)	Gross profit	80%
(Less)	Total operating expenses	30%
(Equals)	Net income	50%

For each dollar of sales 20 cents of it represents a cost of goods sold by Jerves Company. For each dollar of sales 50 cents represent profit or net income realized by Jerves.

These percentages can be used in comparing other companies in the same industry to Jerves.

CLOSING ENTRIES (CLEARING ENTRIES)

At the end of an accounting period you take all the temporary accounts (revenue, expense, and drawing) and summarize their effects on capital or owner equity. To this one must journalize and then post the closing entries to the ledger.

All temporary accounts will then have a *zero balance* when the new accounting period begins.

Permanent accounts: assets, liabilities, capital (owner equity)

Temporary accounts: revenue, expenses, drawing income summary (expense and revenue summary)

(See income summary)

Closing Entries (Clearing Entries)*

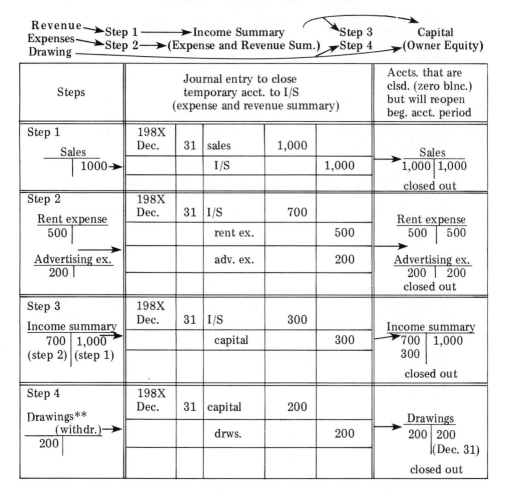

Steps	Journal entry to close temporary acct. to I/S (expense and revenue summary)					Accts. that are clsd. (zero blnc.) but will reopen beg. acct. period
Step 1 Sales ‾‾‾‾ ⎮ 1000→	198X Dec.	31	sales I/S	1,000	 1,000	Sales ‾‾‾‾ 1,000 ⎮ 1,000 closed out
Step 2 Rent expense 500 ⎮ Advertising ex. 200 ⎮	198X Dec.	31	I/S rent ex. adv. ex.	700	 500 200	Rent expense 500 ⎮ 500 Advertising ex. 200 ⎮ 200 closed out
Step 3 Income summary 700 ⎮ 1,000→ (step 2) ⎮ (step 1)	198X Dec.	31	I/S capital	300	 300	Income summary →700 ⎮ 1,000 300 ⎮ closed out
Step 4 Drawings** (withdr.)→ 200 ⎮	198X Dec.	31	capital drws.	200	 200	Drawings 200 ⎮ 200 ⎮(Dec. 31) closed out

*If we are doing closing entries for a corporation we would use retained earnings instead of capital.
**Withdrawals are closed since they represent a nonbusiness expense directly to capital.

COMMON STOCK (CAPITAL STOCK)

It is the capital account which summarizes the amount of assets stockholders have invested in the company.

To the investors:

One type of stock (or piece of paper(s) called stock certificates) which *shows* the amount of *ownership and rights* one has in a corporation.

The rights usually deal with:

1. Right of one to vote in a corporation
2. Right to share in a corporation profit
3. Preemptive right (see definition of preemptive right for more detail)
4. The liquidation process (see liquidation for more detail)

People owning common stock in a company usually have equal rights.

To a corporation:

This is usually a means or way of raising money (capital) by selling shares of stock to investors.

Common Stock (Capital Stock)

Moore Company issued 1,000 share of $10 par common stock to investors at $30 per share.

A. *To an Investor*

> One now has bought ownership and rights into Moore Company (depending on amount bought).

B. *To the Corporation*

> Moore Company has raised $30,000 (1,000 shares X $30 per share) by selling common stock.

56

COMPARATIVE STATEMENTS

Putting reports or statements about a company side by side for two or more periods of time for analysis.

This is done to hopefully interpret or better understand the operation and financial position of a company for a specific *period of time* (income statement) or as of a *certain date* (balance sheet).

(See horizontal and vertical for analysis of comparative statements)

Comparative Statements

Joe's Market Comparative Statement For Years Ended Dec. 31, 198X and 199X		
	199X	198X
Sales	$2,000	$1,900
Sales returns and allowances	200	100
Net sales	1,800	1,800
Cost of goods sold	1,400	1,200
Gross profit	400	600
Total operating expenses	300	500
Net income	$ 100	$ 100

Although both years show *same profit* compare operating expenses, cost of goods sold, and sales returns and allowances to possibly make some analysis between the two years.

COMPOUND JOURNAL ENTRY

The journal entry in which the transaction is recorded (or placed) into a journal with more than two entries. Debits at the margin, credits indented.

Compound Journal Entry

Date		Account Title	Folio (PR)	Debit	Credit
197X May	1	Cash	1	1,000	
		Supplies	4	50	
		Capital—Gary Wood	10		1,050

3 Accounts

COMPUTER

A machine or device which can accept instructions and data (in a form that the machine can translate) in order to process these instructions and data to achieve a desired result (output) or goal.

The five main parts of a computer are:

1. Storage—where data and instructions are kept.
2. Arithmetic/logic—the process area where adding, subtracting, and logic (greater, less than, etc.) are done.
3. Control—the computer "brain" that handles scheduling as well as computer problems that may come up in operations.
4. Input—information or data being "placed" or "fed" into the computer for processing.
5. Output—information or data that has been processed by the computer.

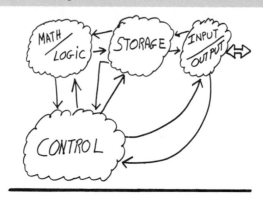

58

COMPUTER PROGRAM

A list of instructions that are written in a language that the computer can accept and translate in order to accomplish a desired result.

These instructions are written by a person called a *programmer*.

Computer Program
(Basic Language)

```
10   Let L   = 1.72
20   Let W   = 2.91
30   Let A   = L*W
40   Let C   = 2*L*2*W
50   Print
60   Print tab* (11); "length is"; L; tab (47) "width is"; W
70   Print
80   Print tab (11); "area is"; A; tab (47); "circumference is"; C
09   End
     Run
```

Desired Result
(What is printed out by the computer)

Length is 1.72   Width is 2.91

Area is 5.0052   Circumference is 9.26

*Tab shows spacing (11 spaces in).

59

CONTINGENT LIABILITY—NOTES RECEIVABLE

The responsibilities to pay a debt or promise of another person if the first person fails to fulfill his promise or obligation.

(See discounted notes receivable)

Contingent Liability—Notes Receivable

	"A" Issues Promissory Note Receivable to "B"	
(1)	Jan. 1	"A" promises in writing to pay "B" $100 on June 1.
	"B" discounts the note receivable	
(2)	Jan. 2	"B" needs money and can't wait until June. "B" goes to bank to exchange note receivable for cash (not the full amount) with a stipulation* that if "A" doesn't pay off promise on June 1, "B" will pay it to the bank. (*"B" is contingently liable for "A."*)
	"A" dishonored note receivable	
(3)	June 1	"A" never pays bill to bank
	Contingent Liability—Notice of Protest	
(4)	June 2	Bank notifies "B" that "B" must pay note receivable that was dishonored by "A."

*This stipulation is not necessary.

CONTRA ACCOUNT (ACCUMULATED DEPRECIATION, ALLOWANCE FOR DOUBTFUL ACCOUNTS)

An account (accumulated depreciation, allowance for doubtful accounts, etc.) which is subtracted from its main or associate account (equipment, accounts receivable) in order to show the net or true book value of the main account on the accounting statements of the company.

A. (Asset) equipment — (contra asset) accumulated depreciation = value of equipment on books

B. (Asset) accounts receivable — (contra asset) allowance for doubtful accounts = what you *expect* to collect or realize from your accounts

(One should be aware that there are other types of contra accounts besides accumulated depreciation and allowance for doubtful accounts.)

Contra Account (Accumulated Depreciation)
Allowance for Doubtful Accounts

Part of Balance Sheet

A. Current assets:

Cash		$21,600
Accounts receivable	$100,000	
Less allowance for doubtful accounts	2,000	98,000

Part of Balance Sheet

B. Plant assets:

Store equipment	$10,200	
Less accumulated depreciation	6,000	$4,200
Office equipment	4,000	
Less accumulated depreciation	2,000	2,000

CONTROLLING ACCOUNT—(ACCOUNTS PAYABLE)

The account in the general ledger (accounts payable) which, after postings are done, shows the *total amount* of dollars we owe people. This one figure is broken down in the subsidiary ledger by showing exactly *who* we owe money to.

The sum of the subsidiary ledger is equal to he one figure in the controlling account (account payable) after postings.

(See accounts payable ledger)

Controlling Account—Accounts Payable

General Ledger

Accounts Payable (511)

Date		Item	Folio (PR)	Debits	Credits	Balance Debits	Credits
Feb.	29		*PJ 1		900		900
	29		*CP 1	400			500

*PJ = Purchase Journal
*CP = Cash Payment Journal

Accounts Payable Ledger*
(Subsidiary)

Cough Brother

Date		Item	Folio (PR)	Debits	Credits	Balance Debits	Credits
Feb.	10		PJ 1		100		100

Ralph Brothers

Date		Item	Folio (PR)	Debits		Balance Debits	Credits
Feb.	8		PJ 1		200		200
	9		CP 1	100			100

Smith Brothers

Date		Item	Folio (PR)	Debits	Credits	Balance Debits	
Feb.	9		PJ 1		600		600
	15		CP 1	300			300

*Not found in general ledger.

CONTROLLING ACCOUNT—(ACCOUNTS RECEIVABLE)

The account in the general ledger (accounts receivable) which, after postings are done, shows the *total amount* of dollars *owed to us.* This one figure is broken down in the subsidiary ledger by showing exactly *who* owes us what.

The sum of the subsidiary ledger is equal to the one figure in the controlling account (account receivable) after postings.

(See accounts receivable ledger)

Controlling Account—Accounts Receivable
General Ledger
Accounts Receivable (140)

Date		Item	Folio (PR)	Debits	Credits	Balance Debits	Credits
Feb.	29		*SJ 1	1,500		1,500	
	29		*CR 1		1,300	200	

*SJ = Sales Journal
*CR = Cash Receipts Journal

Accts. Receivable*—(Subsidairy) Ledger

Bush and Bee Inc.

Date		Item	Folio (PR)	Debits	Credits	Balance Debits	Credits
Feb.	10		SJ 1	500		500	
	18		CR 1		500	——	——

Miller and Company

Date		Item	Folio (PR)	Debits	Credits	Balance Debits	Credits
Feb.	4		SJ 1	750		750	
	8		CR 1		550	200	

Mitchell and Mark Inc.

Date		Item	Folio (PR)	Debits	Credits	Balance Debits	Credits
Feb.	8		SJ 1	250		250	
	15		CR 1		250	——	——

*Not found in general ledger.

CONVERTIBLE BOND

Bonds which may be changed or exchanged for a certain number of shares of stock in the same corporation.

This feature sometimes makes the purchase of these bonds more attractive if the investor thinks the stock price will rise in the future.

Courtesy of E.F. Hutton.

CORPORATION

A company which is considered separate and distinct from its owners (the stockholders) in the eyes of the law.

The company is like an artificial person.

(See business entity for illustration)

Corporations

Advantage: Limited liability
Easier to raise capital
Going concern.

COST OF GOODS SOLD (COST OF SALES)—
MERCHANDISE COMPANY

The part of an income statement which shows the *"cost of the merchandise (goods)"* a company sold in a specific period of time.

This section is a reduction from revenue (sales) because it shows the *cost to the seller* for the merchandise sold.

We are matching the earned sales of merchandise against the costs and expenses incurred to sell that merchandise.

The difference between revenue and cost of the goods sold is gross profit.

(See accrual basis)

Cost of Goods Sold (Cost of Sales)
A Portion of an Income Statement
Jeep's Apple Market

Sales			XXX
Less Cost of Goods Sold			
1. Beginning inventory 198X			$2,000
2. + Purchases		$ 400	
3. − Purchase returns		200	
4. = Net purchases			200
5. Cost of goods available to sell to customers		$2,200	
6. − Ending inventory 198X		1,000	
Cost of goods sold			$1,200

Explanation

1. Cost of apples in store (to Jeeps) to start new period of time.
2. Jeeps bought $400 of apples from a farm to *resell* them to customers.
3. Jeeps returned $200 worth of apples, because they were full of worms, to the farm.
4. Actually Jeeps only bought $200 worth of apples after deducting the wormy apples that were returned.
5. Jeeps has $2,200 worth of apples to sell to his customers (this is a cost to Jeeps). You can be sure Jeeps will sell these apples to his customers for a higher price.
6. Out of $2,200 worth of apples $1,000 worth were not sold. This $1,000 of ending inventory will become the beginning inventory for the next period of time.

65

COST OR MARKET

A traditional accounting practice of pricing ending inventory at what it cost or at the current market price (replacement cost)—whichever one is lower. This practice is based on the accounting principle of conservatism.

Cost or Market

Soap	Cost per Carton to Store	Original Cost to Store	Going Market Rate Now	Cost to Store at Mkt. Rate	Lower of Cost or Market
10 cartons	$5.00	$50.00	$6.00	$60.00	$50.00

Based on this practice the store would price ending inventory at $50 (cost)

COST PRINCIPLE

Record whatever you buy at the price you *paid for it* not at the price you *think* its worth. Record at transaction price. The cost principle helps in verifying transaction records if needed.

COUPON BONDS (BEARER BONDS)

The company issuing coupon bonds usually *does not keep* a record of the names and addresses of each bondholder.

There are interest coupons that are attached onto the bond. Whoever is in possession of the bond at the time of interest presents a coupon to the company's bank for payment.

Coupon Bonds

Bob Finicharro, owner of a coupon bond transferred ownership of his bond to Paula Corman.

Paula did not have to notify the company because when *interest payments* were due she went to the bank and presented a coupon (which was attached to the bond) *no questions asked.*

(See registered bond for comparison)

CREDIT* (DEBIT, CREDIT)

The right side of *any* account or number which is entered on the right side of an account.

(See rules of debits and credits)

Credit

Accounts Payable   Account No. 10

Date	Explanation	Folio (PR)	Debit	Date	Explanation	Fol. (PR)	Credit
				198X Sept. 1	Balance		1 0 0 00

(See foldout chart at end of book
for specific credit rules)

*From Latin derivation credere.

CREDIT MEMORANDUM

A form or piece of paper which is used to notify the buyer or seller or merchandise that adjustments are needed on the purchase or sale of merchandise due to pricing mistakes, wrong deliveries, billing errors, damages, etc. The adjustments are made in the form of a *debit or credit memorandum.*

Allied wholesalers had sold 10 cases of soup to Trembly Inc. on account. After the soup was shipped, Allied realized one case of soup was defective.

Allied issued a credit memo to Trembly which resulted in Allied reducing its sales and reducing accounts receivable (Trembly didn't owe as much).

(See debit memorandum)
General Journal

When a credit memo is issued the result will be to debit sales returns and allowances and credit accounts receivable. (This results on the seller's books.)

On the books of the buyer who receives the credit memo, the result will be to debit accounts payable and credit purchase returns and allowances.

Credit Memorandum

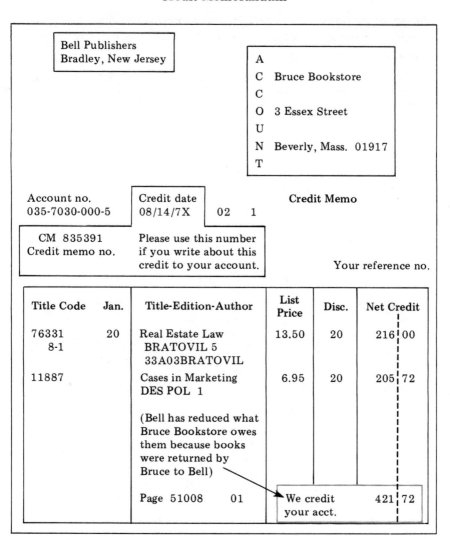

Bell Publishers
Bradley, New Jersey

```
A
C   Bruce Bookstore
C
O   3 Essex Street
U
N   Beverly, Mass.  01917
T
```

| Account no. 035-7030-000-5 | Credit date 08/14/7X   02   1 | Credit Memo |

CM 835391
Credit memo no.

Please use this number
if you write about this
credit to your account.

Your reference no.

Title Code	Jan.	Title-Edition-Author	List Price	Disc.	Net Credit
76331 8-1	20	Real Estate Law BRATOVIL 5 33A03BRATOVIL	13.50	20	216 00
11887		Cases in Marketing DES POL 1	6.95	20	205 72
		(Bell has reduced what Bruce Bookstore owes them because books were returned by Bruce to Bell)			
		Page 51008 01	We credit your acct.		421 72

CREDITORS

People we owe money to for services or commodities (a debt).

We say we have created a liability by borrowing money or buying an asset on account.

These people (creditors) have rights to the assets or things owned by the business to the extent of the debt we owe them.

Creditors

I needed ten dollars for a date.
I went to my best friend.
He lent me the money.
Today he is not my best friend.
He charged me a buck in interest for
The use of his money, that "Dirty *Creditor.*"

CUMULATIVE PREFERRED STOCK

A type of stock which usually gives to the investor a definite or certain amount of dividends each year.

If for some reason the dividends are not paid (in arrears) that year or in past years, the holders of cumulative preferred stock *are entitled* to the past or present dividends when future dividends are paid (or before future dividends are paid).

(See noncumulative preferred stock)

Cumulative Preferred Stock

Barry Bluth bought 100 shares of cumulative preferred stock of Biby Corporation through his local home town stockbroker.

The stockbroker had told Barry that this type of stock will pay him a $100 dividend per year.

If the company fails (in arrears) to pay the dividends, Barry will have rights to the past, as well as the present dividends before other types of stockholders (common) in Biby Corporation are paid.

CURRENT ASSETS

Cash or other assets (or things owned by a business) which a company expects to be turned into cash or sold, or used up within a year or less through the regular operations of the business.

Example ——Accounts receivable
          Supplies
          Cash
          Prepaid rent
          Inventories

(See: Classified balance sheet, marketable securities, notes receivable)

Current Assets
A portion of a balance sheet

Assets		
Current Assets:		
Cash	$ 500	
Accounts receivable	100	
Supplies	200	
Prepaid insurance	300	
Merchandise inventory	500	
Total current assets		$ 1,600

CURRENT LIABILITIES

Obligations or services that we *owe* that will come due or will be fulfilled within *a year or less.*

(See notes payable, accounts payable, salaries payable, long-term liabilities)

Current Liabilities

Mike bought a dozen roses for his girl and charged them (promised to pay later). Thus creating a current liability.

CURRENT RATIO

The total of current assets (cash, supplies, account receivable, etc.) divided by current liabilities (account payable, etc.).

If $\dfrac{current\ assets}{current\ liabilities}$ equaled 2 it would mean that for each $2 of current assets there is one dollar of current liabilities in the business. Current ratio measures a firm's ability to pay its debts.

(See classified balance sheet for current assets and current liabilities)

Current Ratio

Apex Bank had a difficult decision to make as to which company (Jacks or Alls) would receive a short-term bank loan.*

One reason for the bank giving the loan to Jacks was because:

	Jacks	*Alls*
Current Ratio	*3:1*	*1:1*

For each dollar of current liabilities Jacks had three dollars of current assets, while Alls had for each dollar of current liabilities only one dollar of current assets.

It appeared Jack was in a much better position to pay off its debts than Alls (at least in the short-term).

Of course, the current ratio was only *one* factor that the bank analyzed. (In order to come to a decision many factors were investigated.)

*Both in the same type of business.

DATE OF DECLARATION

Day or date that the board of directors of a company *announces its intention* to pay a dividend.

Once this is done the company has created a *liability* or it now owes the dividend.

Date of Declaration

January 8: The board of directors of Doran Corporation declared (announced) a 50 cents cash dividend on its common stock (1,000 shares) payable on February 18 to stockholders of record on January 20. This *creates* a liability (or what they owe) by Doran Corporation to certain stockholders.

The following entry was made to show the declaration of the dividend:

Journal   Page #1

Date		Description (Accounts)	Folio (PR)	Debit	Credit
198X					
Jan.	8	Retained earnings	3	500	
		Cash dividends payable	8		500

(See date of payment for comparison)

73

DATE OF PAYMENT

Date of Payment

January 8: The board of directors of Doran Corporation declared (announced) a 50 cents cash dividend on its common stock (1,000 shares) payable on February 18 to stockholders of record on January 20. When the dividend is paid, the liability (cash dividends payable) will be reduced by paying cash.

The following entry was made on February 18 to show the payment

Journal   Page #2

Date	Description (Accounts)	Folio (PR)	Debit	Credit
198X				
Feb. 18	Cash dividends payable	8	500	
	Cash	1		500

DATE OF RECORD

Date of Record

January 8: The board of directors of Doran Corporation declared (announced) a 50 cent cash dividend on its common stock (1,000 shares) payable on February 18 to *stockholders of record on January 20.*

The common stockholders, on the company's list (or records), on January 20 will receive the 50¢ dividend per share on February 18 (date of payment).

DAYS IN A MONTH RULE

Thirty days has September, April, June, and November; all the rest have 31 except February, which has 28 and 29 during leap year.

DEBENTURE BONDS

The investor buys this type of bond based on the *general credit or reliability of the corporation.*

Bonds which are sold by a company *are not backed up or secured* by any asset (building, equipment, etc.) of the company or other companies.

This becomes important if the company fails to pay off the bond when it comes due.

Debenture Bonds

Jill Hester, holder of a debenture bond, was quite upset when the company failed to honor its obligation.

Jill went to her lawyer who told her that the bond *was not* backed up or secured (since it was a debenture bond) and that he really could not help her. Eventually the corporation went bankrupt and settled on 27¢ on the dollar.

DEBIT (DEBITS, CREDITS)

Left side of *any* account (or number entered on left side on an account).

(See rules of debits and credits)

Debit*

Cash   Account No. 1

Date		Explanation	Fol. (PR)	Debit	Date	Explanation	Fol. (PR)	Credit
198X								
Sept.	1	Balance		1 0 0 00				

(See foldout chart at the end of text for
applying debit rule to specific accounts)

*From the latin debere.

DEBIT MEMORANDUM

A form which is used to notify the buyer or seller of merchandise that *adjustments* are needed on the purchase or sale or merchandise due to pricing mistakes, wrong items delivered, billing errors, damaged, etc. The adjustments are made in the form of *debit or credit memorandum.*

Tremblay Inc., bought 10 cases of soup from Allied Wholesalers on account. After the soup was received, Tremblay realized one case was defective.

Tremblay sent a debit memorandum to Allied, which resulted in Tremblay debiting accounts payable (reducing what he owed) and crediting purchase returns.

(See credit memorandum)
General Journal
Debit Memorandum

Bell Publishers   Bradley, New Jersey

A
C   Bruce Bookstore
C
O   3 Essex Street   MD 19491
U
N   Beverly, Mass. 01915
T

Memorandum	Date	Account No.	Charge
of debit	11-30-72	35-07030	$338.44

Your account has been charged under this MD number. We will continue to show this charge on your statement until your payment is received or credit is processed.

Your Check No.	Date	Amount of	Your Charge Back #	Dated
4905	11-17-72	$13,519.44	None	----------
		Amt. Ded.		
		$338.44		

This charge represents

☒ Returns not credited yet   ☐ Postage
   BX334464
                                    ☐ Duplicate deduction of _____
☐ Price or discount difference
                                    ☐ Your deduction, please send
☐ Underpayment   details

(See credit memorandum for journal entry)

DECLINING-BALANCE METHOD OF DEPRECIATION

A method used to spread (or allocate) the total amount of depreciation related to a plant asset (equipment, building, etc.) over its estimated life.

This method takes *more, or accelerates depreciation* expense in the early or beginning years (as compared with straight-line) of the estimated life or the plant asset.

This method *does not* consider salvage in its calculations, except that under this method the plant asset is usually not *depreciated beyond* whatever the *estimated salvage value is.*

(See sum-of-the-years digit method)

Declining-Balance Method of Depreciation

Facts:
1. Cost of truck $5,000
2. 4-year life
3. Rate is 50% (25% is straight-line) or twice straight-line rate
4. At end of 4th year residual value is approximately $300

Year	Cost	Accum. Depr. at Beginning of Year	Book Value at Beg. of Year (Cost-acc. dep)	Deprec. (Book Val. at Beg. of Yr. Times R)	Acc. Depr. at End of Year	Book Value at End of Year (cost-acc. dep.)
1	$5,000	0	$5,000 (5,000 − 0) (cost-acc. dep.)	$2,500 (5,000 X 50%)	$2,500	$2,500 (cost-acc. dep.) (5,000 − 2,500)
2	$5,000	2,500 (acc. depr. end of yr. 1)	2,500 (5,000 − 2,500) (cost-acc. dep.)	1,250 (2,500 X 50%)	3,750 (2,500 + 1,250)	1,250 (5,000 − 3,750)
3	$5,000	3,750	1,250 (5,000 − 3,750)	625 (50% X 1,250)	4,375 (3,750 + 625)	625 (5,000 − 4,375)
4	$5,000	4,375	625 (5,000 − 4,375)	312.50 (50% X 625)	4,687.50 (4,375 + 312.50)	$312.50

We have not gone below $300.

DEFAULTING—NOTES RECEIVABLE

The process when one who had promised to pay (the maker) a note receivable fails to fulfill his promise at the maturity date. This is called *defaulting.*

(See maker, contingent liability)

Defaulting—Notes Receivable

On June 2 the Bull Bank notified Jim Driscoll that he must pay a note receivable due to the fact Joe Walker defaulted (or dishonored his note).

This defaulting meant that Joe didn't pay off his promise when it came due, with the bank turning to Jim Driscoll (who was contingently liable) for payment.

DEFERRAL

Two types:

1. *Postponing*—the recognition of a sale (although you have already received the money) until you earn it.

2. *Postponing*—the recognition of an expense (although you have already paid for the expense) until you use it up (the asset that is).

(See accrued expense, accrued revenue)

Deferral

January 1: Spice Magazine received $100 from Pam Sisto for payment of a one year subscription to *Spice*.

Since Spice Magazine hadn't really earned *any* of the sale (until they start sending the magazine) the following entry was recorded by Spice:

Journal   Page #2

Date	Description (Accounts)	Folio (PR)	Debit	Credit
198X Dec. 31	Cash	1	100	
	Unearned revenue	10		100

Unearned revenue is a liability—Spice *owes* a service to Pam Sisto (a *liability* called unearned revenue). Unearned revenue is a *liability* and not revenue.

When Spice earns the sale, or part of the sale, they will reduce their liability (by a debit to unearned revenue) and will show a sale (a credit to earned revenue).

Remember unearned revenue is a liability.

Spice postpones the recognition of a sale until they *earn* it.

DEFICIT—RETAINED EARNINGS

When retained earnings has a debit balance. It is called a deficit.

(See retained earnings)

Deficit—Retained Earnings

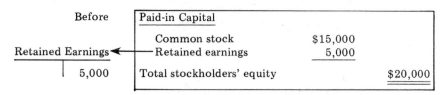

	Paid-in Capital		
	Common stock	$15,000	
Retained Earnings	Retained earnings	5,000	
5,000	Total stockholders' equity		$20,000

After an $8,000 reduction in retained earnings:

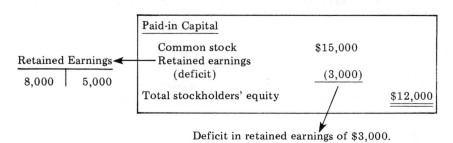

	Paid-in Capital		
	Common stock	$15,000	
Retained Earnings	Retained earnings		
	(deficit)	(3,000)	
8,000 | 5,000	Total stockholders' equity		$12,000

Deficit in retained earnings of $3,000.

DEPARTMENTAL MARGIN (CONTRIBUTION MARGIN)

The amount of revenue that an *individual* department in a company contributed or adds to the operations of the overall company.

This amount is calculated as follows:

	Revenue
(Less)	Cost of goods sold
	Gross Profit
(Less)	Direct expenses (related to that department)
	Departmental margin (amount of revenue contributed by that department)

Department Margin (Contribution Margin)

Val Company Portion of an Income Statement for Year Ended December 31, 197X			
	Sweaters	Sporting Goods	Total
Sales	$20,000	$30,000	$50,000
Cost of goods sold	15,000	20,000	35,000
Gross profit on sales	5,000	10,000	15,000
Direct expenses	3,000	2,000	5,000
Department margin	2,000	8,000	10,000

Out of the $10,000 contributed by the two departments (before indirect expenses—rent, lights, etc.) sporting goods was responsible for $8,000 or 80% of the total company.

DEPLETION

The cost or expense of exhausted resources (mineral, ore, etc.) which are taken from the land.

DEPRECIATION

The spreading out of the *original cost* over the estimated life of the tangible asset.

(See accumulated depreciation)

Depreciation

Earl Miller Inc. bought a car for $2,000. At the end of the first year the accountant told Earl to take depreciation on the car for $500.

Car minus accumulated depreciation equals book value of car.

$$\$2,000 - \$500 = \$1,500$$

Insight: Earl told the accountant the car was still as good as new. "So what," said the accountant "depreciation is only a paper entry which will give you more business expenses (when depreciation is taken it is an expense) and your company a tax break."

DIRECT LABOR (MANUFACTURING BUSINESS)

Cost of labor (work) which can be *directly related and is specifically charged* to certain products that are manufactured (or produced).

DIRECT MATERIALS (MANUFACTURING BUSINESS)

Cost of material which can be directly related (because it becomes a part of the product) and is specifically charged to certain products that are manufactured (or produced).

DIRECT WRITE-OFF METHOD FOR BAD DEBTS

When a company has decided that a customer will not pay his bill they consider the customer to be a bad debt (an expense) and *at this time* shows this expense (or loss) in their accounting books.

This direct method *doesn't try to estimate* what a company's bad debts will be (see allowance method) but this method waits until the bad debt(s) happens.

Direct Write-Off Method for Bad Debts*

Belle Supermarket usually makes *most* of its sales for cash (therefore, the store doesn't try to estimate bad debts).

On January 8 Joe Frank came into the store and asked if he could charge food ($100) due to financial troubles.

The manager, married to Joe's sister, approved the charge.

Three months later, the manager gave up trying to collect the money and called Joe a bad debt expense. The following entry was recorded:

Journal   Page #1

Date		Description (Accounts)	Folio (PR)	Debit	Credit
198X March	8	Uncollectable account exp.**	10	100	
		Accounts rec.-Joe Frank	5		100

Key Point: This method often overstates revenue in period of time sale is made but understates earnings in the period of time the bad debt is recognized.

---

*The direct method doesn't use the account entitled allowances for doubtful accounts.
**Some texts use bad debt expense instead of uncollectable account expense.

DISCOUNT ON STOCK

The result of selling stock (or issuing stock) at a price that is *less* than par value.

(See par value for further help)

Discount on Stock

On December 1, 197X the Abby Corporation issued 500 shares of $10 par common stock at $8 per share.

The following entry was made on the company books:

Journal   Page #1

Date		Description (Accounts)	Folio (PR)	Debit	Credit
198X Dec.	1	Cash	1	4,000*	
		Discount common stock	18	1,000**	
		Common stock	17		5,000

(500 shares
x $10 par)

(See premium on stock for comparison)

Key Point: Discount on stock is an account with a debit balance found in the stockholder's equity section of the balance sheet.

*500 shares x $8 or $4,000.
**Discount on stock was $2 per share or $1,000.

DISCOUNTED NOTES RECEIVABLE

Usually a person or a company who owns a note but *needs or wants money now* (can't wait until the maturity date) goes to a bank or finance company to *exchange* the note for cash (which is less than what would have been received at maturity).

When this happens, it is said that the note has been *discounted* by the bank.

Discounted Notes Receivable

John Wills, on December 1, 198X discounted a $1,000 6% 60 day notes receivable dated November 1, 198X with the bank at a discount rate of 8%.

Goal of problem

How much money will John get from the bank?

Steps	Explanation
Step 1-Find maturity value 1. Face value of note = $1,000 + interest on note = 10 maturity value = $1,010	Maturity value = what the bank will receive when the person or company (maker) pays off the note on December 30. (Nov. 1-Dec. 30 = 60 days)
Step 2-Find discount Dec. 1 to Dec. 30 = 30 days	Discount time = the number of days the bank will have to wait until the note comes due (after taking the note from John). This number of days helps the bank figure what it should charge John for discounting the note.
Step 3-Find discount on maturity value $6.73 (8% × $\frac{30}{360}$ × $1,010)	Discount = amount bank charges for waiting 30 days for the note to come due. This discount is based on a rate time number of days before note is paid times maturity value.
Step 4-Find proceeds $1,003.27 $1,010. − $6.73 = $1,003.27 $\binom{\text{Maturity—Discount}}{\text{value \quad on note}}$	What John gets when he discounts the note. John settled for $1,003.27 instead of $1,010 if he could have waited until Dec. 30 and not discounted the note.

DISHONORED NOTES RECEIVABLE

Failure or refusal of a person (maker) to pay a note (or what he owes) when it is due (maturity date).

Dishonored Notes Receivable

On March 1, John Scrivano promised, in writing, to pay to the order of Ken Phillips $100 on June 1 of that same year.

On June 1, the note had now been *dishonored* by Scrivano, who had no intention to pay back Ken Phillips.

DIVIDEND

The share of profits in the form of cash, or company stock, or property, etc., that a corporation divides or gives out to the stockholders of the corporation (each type of stock *may receive* different amounts of dividends).

This amount is determined by the corporations board of directors. A dividend does not have to be paid each year.

(See cash dividends and stock dividends for more detail)

DIVIDEND IN ARREARS

Dividends which are owed to cummulative preferred stockholders that have *not been paid* by the company.

(See cumulative preferred stock for further help)

Dividend in Arrears

Neal Goldman bought 100 shares of *cumulative preferred stock* of
APC Corporation through his local home town stockbrocker.

The stockbroker had told Neal that this type of stock will pay him a
$100 dividend per year.

If the company fails or is late (in arrears) in paying the dividend,
Neal *will have rights to the past as well as present* dividends before
other types of stock (common stock) are paid.

DOUBLE-ENTRY BOOKKEEPING

The idea in accounting that requires that *each transaction* be recorded *in at least two accounts* (the result being the total of the debits is equal to the total of the credits).

(See bookkeeping, rules of debits and credits, accounting equation)

Double-Entry Bookkeeping

Jan. 8 Bopel Motors bought a car from GMV Corporation for $3,000 (for resale to its customers).

The following entry was recorded in Bopel's journal:

Journal   Page #1

Date		Description (Accounts)	Folio (PR)	Debit	Credit
198X Jan.	8	Purchases	500	3,000	
		Cash	1		3,000

The general ledger (when posted) shows:

General Ledger

Cash (1)

Date		Item	Folio (PR)	Debits	Credits	Balance Debits	Credits
198X Jan.	1		1	5,000		5,000	
	8		1		3,000	2,000	

Purchases (500)

Date		Item	Folio (PR)	Debits	Credits	Balance Debits	Credits
198X Jan.	8			3,000		3,000	

EARNINGS PER SHARE

A calculation which shows how much profit or earnings the corporation is making per share (or for each share) of stock.

$$\frac{Total\ profit\ (net\ income)\ after\ taxes}{Total\ number\ of\ shares\ of\ stock\ (outstanding)}$$

Earnings Per Share

"Special News Release"

It was reported by Duane Dell, president of Toyland Inc., that 197X was a record year for sales and earnings.

Mr. Dell reported sales reached $500,000 with net income hitting an all time high of $200,000 after taxes.

Duane went on to say that since the company had only 100,000 shares of stock outstanding, the companies showed *earnings per share of $2* $\frac{(200,000\ NI).}{100,000\ shares}$

EMPLOYEE

A person who is hired (employed) by a company or person for wages or salary.

Employee

Jeff Frank works for Mingle Motors as a mechanic. Jeff is an *employee* of Mingle Motors.

(See employer)

EMPLOYER

A person or company who hires (employs) others to work in a company for wages or salary.

Employer

Stop and Hop, a corporation, is the *employer* of many thousands of workers (stock clerks, managers, meatmen, etc.).

(See employee)

EMPLOYEE'S EARNING RECORD

A form which contains all the payroll information that has been *accumulating or building up* about an employee or worker in a business for the *calendar year* (January 1 to December 31).

(See: employers payroll taxes, net pay [for employee taxes])

Employee's Earning Record

Employee's Name Darlene Malawka   Social Security Number 021-36-9494   Employee Number   5

Home Address 17 Andrew Road   In Case of Emergency Murray Slater   Home Number (Phone) 289-2334

Employed 9/1/70   Termination _____   Male ____ Married X

Date of Birth May 20, 1947   Date Becomes 65 May 20, 2012   Female X   Single ____

Occupation Sales person   Number of Exemptions 4

Pay Rate $3.45

Date		Time Lost			Time Work											

Per Ends	Paid	Hrs. Reason	Total	O.T. Hrs.	Reg. Pay	O.T. Prem. Pay	Gross Pay	F.I.C.A. Taxes	Fed. Incm. Tax	Medical Ins.	Union Dues	Total Deduc.	Net Pay	Check Number	Cumulative Pay
1/8		40			$138		$138	$6.90	$10.70	$4.00	$2.50	$24.10	$113.90	103	$138
1/15		40			$138		$138	$6.90	$10.70	$4.00	$2.50	$24.10	$113.90	190	$276
Totals															

The earnings record is broken into 4   13-week quarters.

EMPLOYER'S PAYROLL TAXES

The employer pays:

1. *FICA (Federal Insurance Contributions Act)*—The employer matches the total amount of FICA contributed by its employees. Congress sets the rate and salary base used in the calculations of FICA.

2. *Federal Unemployment Compensation*—the employer pays the tax. The employee does not. This tax is to help people who have become unemployed.

3. *State Unemployment Compensation Tax*—the employer pays the tax. The worker does not. If the employer has provided stable employment to his workers the business in some states receives a reduced rate.

(See employee's earning record, payroll register)

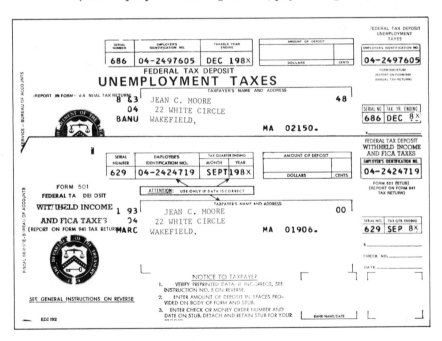

Employers payroll tax expense equals the sum of (1) FICA of employer, (2) Federal Unemployment, and (3) State Unemployment.

ENDING INVENTORY—MERCHANDISE COMPANY

The amount of goods (merchandise) on hand in a company at the end of an accounting period.

It is this ending inventory that will become the beginning inventory in the next accounting period.

(See beginning inventory, cost of goods sold. For calculating ending inventory, see LIFO, FIFO, weighted average, gross profit method, or retail method)

Ending Inventory—Merchandise Company

This figure of ending inventory ($22,150) shows the cost to Jim's Supermarket for the goods (merchandise on the shelf or in the back room) that was *not* sold to its customer during an accounting period.

This cost of ending merchandise is subtracted from the cost of the goods available for sale.

This ending inventory becomes the beginning inventory in the next accounting period (then it will become a part of the cost of the goods sold by Jim's Supermarket).

Jim's Supermarket
Income Statement
for Year Ended December 31, 198X

Revenue from sales:

Sales		$267,736	
Less: Sales returns and allowances	$ 2,140		
Sales discount	1,822	3,962	
Net Sales			$263,774

Cost of merchandise sold:

Merchandise inv. Jan. 1, 198X (beg. inv.)*		$ 19,700	
Purchases	$205,280		
Less purchases discount	1,525		
Net purchases		203,755	
Merchandise available for sale		223,455	
Less ending merchandise inv. Dec. 31, 198X**		22,150	
Cost of merchandise sold.			201,305

Gross profit on sales. . . . . $ 62,469

*Assumed sold and thus a cost.
**Assumed not sold and thus becomes beginning inventory.

94

EQUITY

The rights or claims of others to things (assets or properties) owned by a business: includes both the rights of the owner (called capital or owner equity) and the rights of the people we owe money to (called creditors or liabilities). The creditors and owner have supplied the assets to the business.

(See accounting equation, balance sheet, stockholders equity)

Equity

Assets = Equities

Liabilities + Capital (owner equity)

EXPENSES

Costs of assets consumed in operating or running a business. A sacrifice (cost) of running a business. Expenses are increased by debits.

(See matching concept)

An expense may be recognized even though not paid. Example: heat house in August, don't pay bill until September—still an expense in August.

EXPIRED COSTS

Costs which have been *used up* (or assets consumed) in running or operating a business.

(See prepaid for further help)

Expired Costs

Mike bought a life insurance policy good for five years (for $20.00). At the end of the first year $4.00 or one-fifth of the insurance, had *expired or been used up.*

Mike now only has four years of life insurance.

EXTRAORDINARY ITEMS

Unusual happenings or transactions in a business that greatly Affect the financial condition of the business.

These unusual transactions are not the typical activities that normally happen in running the operations of the business.

(See transactions for details)

FACTORY OVERHEAD—MANUFACTURING BUSINESS

Costs in a manufacturing business that do not relate directly into the making of the finished product.

Factory overhead equals the total of all manufacturing costs in a company minus the sum of direct material and direct labor include rent, heat, insurance, etc.

Note: Raw materials and direct labor are not included in factory overhead.

FICA*
FEDERAL INSURANCE CONTRIBUTION ACT

A deduction from a persons gross pay which is used for federal programs involving the aged, health insurance, disabilities, etc.

The employer is required to match the FICA contribution of the employee.

There is a maximum that can be deducted each year based on a percentage of the earnings (as determined by Congress).

(See employer's payroll taxes, gross pay, net pay, payroll register)

*If worker A earns $40,000 and worker B earns $100,000, both pay same amount of FICA in the same calendar year.

FINISHED GOODS INVENTORY ACCOUNT—
MANUFACTURING COMPANY

One type* of inventory account in a manufacturing business that contains cases of goods or merchandise that are *ready* to be sold.

The costs of direct materials, direct labor, and factor overhead make up the cost of *finished goods*.

(See direct labor and factory overhead)

Key Point: Finished goods inventory is a current asset on the balance sheet.

*The other two types of inventory: 1. raw materials; 2. work in process (goods in process).

FIRST-IN, FIRST-OUT (FIFO)

A method used to assign or place a cost or dollar figure on the ending inventory in a business.

This method assumes the ending inventory is *made up of the latest or most recently purchased items.*

It is assumed that the first stuff brought into a store will be the first stuff sold.

The flow assumes that the *old merchandise in a store is sold before the new. So if anything is left in the store at the end of a period of time, we assume it is the newer merchandise.*

(See LIFO, and weighted average)

First-In, First-Out
J. J. Supermarket

Old	No. of Cans of Soup Bought for Resale (to Customers)	Cost Per Can	Total Cost
On January 1, 198X	20	$3.00	$ 60.00
March 1	15	2.00	30.00
November 3	10	1.00	10.00
November 10	55	2.00	110.00
New	100		$210.00

If at the end of the year 10 cans of soup are left in the store, the cost of these cans are calculated as follows:

$2.00 X 10 cans = $20.00
Cost of ending inventory ────► Cost of goods sold = $190

(See weighted average and last-in, first-out for comparison)

99

FISCAL YEAR

One complete year in accounting. The year can start at *any* time but must meet the requirement of 12 consecutive months. Many companies use January 1 to December 31. But, to repeat, it is not mandatory to start the year on January 1. A fiscal year could fall on the same time as a natural business year. For example, a car dealers business year is October 1 to September 30.

(See calendar year for comparison)

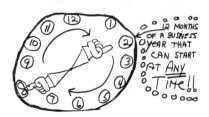

FIXED ASSETS (PLANT ASSETS, TANGIBLE ASSETS, NONCURRENT ASSETS)

Things of value owned by a business (usually *not* for resale) that have a *long life* can be used in the production or sale of other assets or services. Assets which will produce revenue for more than one fiscal period.

Examples include: building, land, and equipment.

(See classified balance sheet)

100

FIXED LIABILITIES

Obligations that we owe that will not be due for a year or more. When they become due within a year, they become current liabilities.

(See classified balance sheet)

Fixed Liabilities

Ed Noon wanted to buy a house. He went to the bank to borrow $15,000.

Ed received the loan with the condition stating his loan would *not come due* for five years.

A *fixed liability* was created.

FOB DESTINATION (FREE ON BOARD)

The seller of the goods *is responsible to pay* the *transportation costs* (freight) involved with getting the good(s) to the buyer (or reaching the buyer's destination). *Usually seller retains ownership until goods are received by purchaser.*

(For comparison, see FOB shipping point)

FOB SHIPPING POINT (FREE ON BOARD)

The *buyer* of the goods *is responsible to pay* the *transportation costs* (freight) involved with getting the good(s) from the seller (or his shipping point). *Usually buyer assumes ownership as soon as goods are shipped.*

(For comparison, see FOB destination)

FREIGHT-IN

An account which shows the *transportation costs* (or shipping charge) the purchaser (buyer) is responsible for.

Freight-in represents a part of the cost of the goods (merchandise) bought or purchased. Some people add the cost of the freight right on to the purchase account. This applies to purchase of merchandise only.

Freight-In

Fred Finger, manager of Toys Inc., bought $500,000 of purchases (or toys for resale to his customers) from a toy wholesaler.

In order to get the toys (purchases) Fred had to pay a shipping (transportation) charge of $1,000.

Fred made the following entry:

Journal   Page #1

Date		Descriptions (Accounts)	Folio (PR)	Debit	Credit
198X Jan.	5	Purchases	10	500.000	
		Freight-in	5	1,000	
		Cash	1		501,000

(Both debits represent a *cost* to Toys Inc. Both accounts will show up on Toy's income statement.)

(See cost of goods sold)

Key Point: Freight-in account is a debit balance which will be found on the income statement.

FUND STATEMENT (CHANGE IN FINANCIAL POSITION)

A report or statement which shows the change in net working capital (current assets minus current liabilities) or funds for a business from one period of time to another.

This report is concerned with changes in liquidity (things which can be quickly turned into cash or quickly used in the operations of the business). To explain the change one analyzes all the noncurrent accounts to see their effect on the current accounts.

A cash flow statement is concerned with the change in the *cash position* of a business from one period of time to another.

(See cash flow, funds for comparison)

Funds Statement (Change in Financial Position)

Bear Corporation
Funds Statement
For Year Ended December 31, 198X

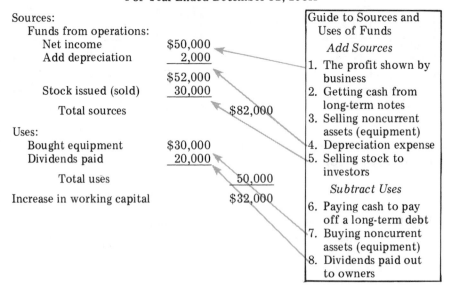

Sources:		Guide to Sources and Uses of Funds
Funds from operations:		*Add Sources*
Net income	$50,000	1. The profit shown by business
Add depreciation	2,000	
	$52,000	2. Getting cash from long-term notes
Stock issued (sold)	30,000	3. Selling noncurrent assets (equipment)
Total sources	$82,000	4. Depreciation expense
Uses:		5. Selling stock to investors
Bought equipment	$30,000	*Subtract Uses*
Dividends paid	20,000	6. Paying cash to pay off a long-term debt
Total uses	50,000	7. Buying noncurrent assets (equipment)
Increase in working capital	$32,000	8. Dividends paid out to owners

FUNDS

(See fund statement)

Funds

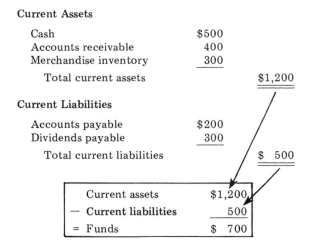

Current Assets

Cash	$500	
Accounts receivable	400	
Merchandise inventory	300	
Total current assets		$1,200

Current Liabilities

Accounts payable	$200	
Dividends payable	300	
Total current liabilities		$ 500

Current assets	$1,200
— Current liabilities	500
= Funds	$ 700

GENERAL JOURNAL

(See: sale, purchase, cash receipts, cash disbursement and check register)

105

General Journal

Date		Account	Folio (PR)	Debit	Credit
19XX Sept.	4	Accounts payable-Ralph Bros.	√ 511	200	
		Purchases returns & allow.	212		200
	9	Sales, returns & allowances	210	500	
		A/R Mitchell and Mark	√ 200		500

Sep. 4 Received a credit memorandum from the Ralph Brothers for defective merchandise, $200 (three postings needed).

Post:

1. To accounts payable (as a debit) in the general ledger. When this is done the account number (511) is put in the post reference column.

2. To Ralph Brothers in our accounts payable subsidiary ledger to show we don't owe Ralph Brothers as much money (because we returned some purchases). When this is done, a check (√) is put in the post reference column.

3. A credit of $200 to purchase returns and allowances in the general ledger. When this is shown, the account number (212) is put in the post reference column.

Sep. 9 Issued to Mitchell and Mark Inc. a credit memorandum for merchandise returned. Credit memo No. 45, $500 (three postings needed).

Post:

1. A debit of $500 to sales returns and allowances in the general ledger. When this is done, the account number (210) is put in the post reference column.

2. To accounts receivable as a credit in the general ledger. When this is done, the account number (200) is put in the post reference column.

3. To Mitchell and Mark in our accounts receivable subsidiary ledger to show they don't owe us as much money (because they returned some goods or services to us). When this is posted, a check (√) is placed in the post reference column.

GENERAL LEDGER (PRINCIPAL LEDGER)

The book or place that contains the income statement and balance sheet accounts. (It is in order of the chart of accounts.)

A list of the general ledger accounts and balances forms a trial balance.

(*See subsidiary ledger for comparison—accounts payable or accounts receivable)

General Ledger (Principal Ledger)**

Cash (1)

Date	Item	Folio (PR)	Debits	Credits	Balance Debits	Credits

Store Supplies (2)

Date	Item	Folio (PR)	Debits	Credits	Balance Debits	Credits

Purchases (500)

Date	Item	Folio (PR)	Debits	Credits	Balance Debits	Credits

*Subsidiary ledgers are not in the general ledger.
**The general ledger is numbered based on account numbers and is not paged as a typical book would be.

GOING CONCERN CONCEPT

An assumption in accounting that a business will function (or not go out of business) for an indefinite or undeterminable number of years.*

(See business entry)

---

*This is one reason why creditors are willing to supply assets to a business and accept payment at a future date.

GOODWILL

The excess amount paid for a company over the value of net assets.

This results when expected future earnings (or earning power) of the company is in excess of the normal or usual rates of return of other companies in that industry.

(See intangible assets)

Why?
Good customer relationships
Location
Employee morale
Product superiority
Managerial skill
Business reputation

Remember goodwill is an intangible asset.

GROSS PAY

The amount of money earned by a worker in wages before all deductions (taxes, social security, etc.) are taken out.

Gross pay is what we wish we could take home.

(See net pay for comparison)

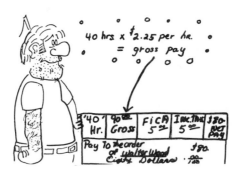

40 hrs x $2.25 per hr. = gross pay

GROSS PROFIT (GROSS MARGIN)

The amount of money *earned** (which is collected or will be collected) from the sale of goods minus the cost of the "goods" we have sold.

(See net sales for more detail)

Gross Profit (Gross Margin)

	Jeep's Apple Market (A Portion of an Income Statement)			
	Revenue			
1.	Gross sales			$5,000
2.	Less: sales returns	$1,000		
3.	Net sales			$4,000
	Cost of Goods Sold			
4.	Beginning inventory 198X		$2,000	
5.	+ Purchases	$400		
6.	− Purchase returns.	200		
7.	Net purchases.		200	
8.	Cost of goods avaliable to sell. . . .		$2,200	
9.	Ending inventory		1,000	
	Cost of goods sold			1,200
10.	Gross profit.			$2,800

*Remember, a sale is a sale, under the accrual method of accounting, when it is earned, whether money is received or not!

Explanation

1. Total dollars spent by customers in buying apples from Jeep's (charge as well as cash) $5,000.

2. Customer returned $1,000 worth of apples due to worms that were found in those apples.

3. Total sales minus the returns by the customers ($4,000).

4. Cost of apples in store (to Jeeps) to start new period of time ($2,000).

5. Jeeps bought $400 of apples from a farm to *resell* to customers.

6. Jeep returned $200 worth of apples because they were full of worms.

7. Actually Jeep only bought $200 worth of apples after deducting wormy apples.

8. Jeep has $2,200 worth of apples to sell to his customers (this is a cost to Jeeps who sells them at a higher price).

9. Out of $2,200 worth of apples $1,000 were not sold. This will become the beginning inventory next period.

10. Before such expenses as heat, wages, etc., Jeeps apple market showed a gross profit of $2,800.

Don't forget, it will be gross profit less operating expenses that will equal net income.

GROSS PROFIT METHOD

A method used by a business to estimate a cost or dollar figure for ending inventory.

This method assumes the business knows its average (usual) gross profit percentage $\dfrac{\text{gross profit}}{\text{net sales}}$ which is used in trying to estimate a figure for ending inventory.

(For comparison see: LIFO, FIFO, weight average, and retail method of costing ending inventory)

Gross Profit Method

Given: Net sales =	$ 5,000
Gross profit =	30% of net sales
Net purchases =	$ 4,000
January 1 beginning inventory =	$10,000

What is the goal? Get an estimated cost of ending inventory on Jan. 31.

Steps:

1. Remember: net sales — cost of goods sold = gross profit
   $1,500 (30% x $5,000)

2. Cost of goods sold equals $3,500 (net sales ($5,000 — gross profit ($1,500)

3. Cost of goods sold equals

	Beginning inventory	$10,000
+	Net purchases	4,000
	Cost of goods available to sell	$14,000
—	Ending inventory	?
=	Cost of goods sold	$ 3,500

4. To reach our goal what number must be subtracted from $14,000 (cost of goods available to sell) in order to get $3,500?

   $14,000 — $10,500 = $3,500

   Estimated cost of ending inventory January 31.

GROSS SALES

The total revenue (cash and/or charge sales) made by a business in running its operations for a specific period of time.

(See accrual and cash basis accounting, gross profit)

Gross Sales

Jim's Supermarket Income Statement for Year Ended December 31, 198X		
Revenue from sales (Gross sales)		$70,000*
Less: Sales discounts	$5,000	
Sales returns & allowances	3,000	8,000
Net sales		$62,000

Gross sales is what Jim wished he had but net sales is what he must be satisfied with.

Key Point:

gross sales
− sales discount
− SRA
= Net Sales

*This could be all cash or partially cash and accounts receivable.

HORIZONTAL ANALYSIS OF STATEMENTS

One way of understanding or interpreting comparative statements.

This method shows the rate and amount change across columns of statements from period to period.

This way will hopefully give a better understanding of the operations and financial position of a company as of a certain date.

(See comparative statements for more detail)

Horizontal Analysis (Across Columns) of Statements

Joe's Market
Comparative Statement
for Years Ended December 31, 197X and 198X

	197X	196X	Am't of Change	Rate*
Sales	$2,000	$1,900	+100	+ 5.26%
Sales returns and allowances	200	100	+100	+100%
Net sales	$1,800	$1,800	0	
Cost of goods sold	1,400	1,200	+200	+16.6%
Gross profit	$ 400	$ 600	−200	−33.3%
Total operating expense	300	500	−200	−40%
Net income	$ 100	$ 100	0	

*Change base 196X

$$5.26\% = \frac{+100}{1,900}$$

114

INCOME STATEMENT (EARNINGS STATEMENT, OPERATING STATEMENT)

Earned revenue (sales) — incurred expenses = profit *or* loss

We match the amount of money earned (which is collected and/or will be collected) from the sale of goods or from services performed, against the expense incurred (or that resulted) in earning that revenue for a specific period of time.

If sales are greater than expenses a profit is made.

If expenses are greater than sales a loss results.

(See matching concept)

Income Statement

John's Cleaners
Income Statement for Year Ended December 31, 198X

Revenue.		$20,000
Operating expense:		
Cleaning wages	$8,000	
Water and electricity.	500	
Rent expense	800	
Cleaning supplies expense	500	
Depreciation expense-cleaning equipment. .	1,000	
Total operating expenses:		10,800
Net income		$ 9,200

For an income statement for a merchandise company see gross profit on p. 110.

INCOME SUMMARY (EXPENSE AND REVENUE SUMMARY) ACCOUNT

The temporary account* to which *all revenues, costs, and expenses* are closed or transferred to at the end of the accounting period.

The balance of income summary account is then closed or transferred to the capital account.

All revenues and expenses, as well as income summary, will then have *zero* balances to start the next accounting period.

*Permanent accounts would be assets, liabilities, capital, retained earnings etc.

(See closing entries)

Income Summary (Expense and revenue summary)

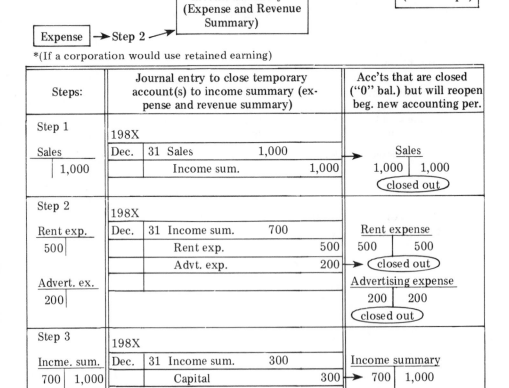

Steps:	Journal entry to close temporary account(s) to income summary (expense and revenue summary)			Acc'ts that are closed ("0" bal.) but will reopen beg. new accounting per.
Step 1 Sales ___ | 1,000	198X Dec. | 31 Sales	1,000		Sales 1,000 | 1,000 ⟨closed out⟩
	| Income sum.		1,000	
Step 2 Rent exp. 500| Advert. ex. 200|	198X Dec. | 31 Income sum.	700		Rent expense 500 | 500 ⟨closed out⟩
	| Rent exp.		500	
	| Advt. exp.		200	Advertising expense 200 | 200 ⟨closed out⟩
Step 3 Incme. sum. 700 | 1,000 step 2 | step 1	198X Dec. | 31 Income sum.	300		Income summary 700 | 1,000 300 ⟨closed out⟩
	| Capital		300	

116

INTANGIBLE ASSETS

Noncurrent assets which have a long life which have no physical appearance which will produce revenue for more than one fiscal period.

(See goodwill)

Intangible Assets

goodwill
trademarks
copyrights
patents
franchises

INTEREST

Cost of using someone else's money.

(See discounting notes receivable)

Interest

Paul needed some money for doing his Christmas shopping.

He went to BC loan company and borrowed $100 for 1 year at a 10% interest rate.

When the loan came due (maturity date) Paul paid BC $110.
($100 + [10% X $100 or $10])

($10 of which was the interest (or the cost of using someone else's money.)

INTERIM STATEMENTS

Statements that are prepared or made *in between or during* the fiscal year (a 12-month period of time).

This is done for management, which wants to know how the company is doing during the year without having to wait 12 months to get the year-end results.

Interim reports may be prepared monthly, or every three months, etc. It depends on the demand of the people wanting the information.

Interim Statement

Neptune Company
Income Statement
for Month Ended June 30, 198X

Sales	$1,000
Less cost of goods sold	500
Gross profit	$ 500
Less operating expenses	200
Net income for month	$ 300

(Since this company makes 12 interim income statements, the final year-end statement will summarize the *12 individual* statements)

INTERNAL CONTROL

A method or system used by a business to control such things as fraud, stolen goods, inaccurate figures, etc., in its operations.

The internal control system (if efficient) allows management to get a "true picture" of its business position at a given point of time.

(See vouchers, check register)

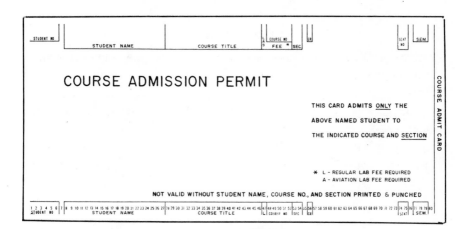

INVOICE

A statement or bill showing a list of all goods and services bought *or* sold.

(See purchase order)

Invoice

TERLIN CORRUGATED BOX CO., INC.	INVOICE
15 RALPH ROAD	
SALEM, MA 01970	NO 5638

TELEPHONE: 745-1174	DATE 11/9/8X
	YOUR
	ORDER NO.

SOLD TO ● RUSSELL SEAFOOD INC.   SHIPPED TO

● 21 ATLANTIC AVENUE

● SALEM, MA   01970

OUR ORDER #1132	SALESMAN	TERMS 1% - 10, NET - 30	FOB DEST.	DATE SHIPPED	SHIPPED VIA
QUANT. ORDER.	QUANTITY SHIPPED	STOCK NO./ DESCRIPTION	UNIT PRICE	UNIT	AMOUNT
	1,400	12-8 OZ. SHRIMP	84	85	M		118	70
	700	12-16 LB. ONION RINGS	158	10	M		110	67
				TOTAL			229	37

119

JOURNAL

Book or place where transactions are *first* put or recorded. The process of putting transactions into a journal is called *journalizing*.

The transactions are placed into the journal in chronological order (January 1, 2, 8, 10 etc.)

The journal links the debit and credit portions of a transaction together.

(See accounting cycle)

Book of
original entry

JOURNAL ENTRY

The transaction that is recorded into a journal. Debits at the margin: credits indented.

Journal Entry

Journal   Page #1

Date		Account Titles	Folio (PR)	Debit	Credit
198X Sept.	1	Office equipment		500	
		Cash			500
		(bought equipment for cash)			

JOURNALIZING TRANSACTIONS

The process of placing or recording transactions in a journal (a book or place where transactions are first put, or recorded) from source documents such as bills, sales slips.

Journalizing Transactions*

Transaction:
Bought truck for business with cash ($1,000).

General Journal

Date		Account Titles	Folio (PR)	Debit	Credit
198X Sept.	1	Truck		1,000	
		Cash			1,000

Don't forget to ask yourself

1. What accounts are affected?
2. What are their categories?
3. Are the accounts increasing or decreases?
4. What are the rules of debit and credit?

*For a special journal sample see cash receipts journal.

121

LAST-IN, FIRST-OUT (LIFO)

A method used to assign or place a cost or dollar figure on the ending inventory in a business.

This method tries to match revenue and expenses by assuming the *newest merchandise in a store is sold before the older merchandise* in the store so if anything is left, we assume it is the *older* merchandise.

The last "stuff" brought into the store is the first "stuff" to be sold.

This method assumes the ending inventory is made up of the *earliest* purchases made by the business.

(See matching concept)

Last-In, First-Out

J.J. Supermarket

Facts:	No. of Cans of Soup Bought for Resale	Cost Per Can	Total Cost
Oldest on Jan. 1, 198X	20	$3.00	$ 60
(Earliest) March 1	15	2.00	30
Nov. 3	10	1.00	10
Nov. 10	55	2.00	110
Newest	100		$210
(Latest)			

If at the end of the year 10 cans of soup are left in the store, the cost of these cans are calculated as follows:

$3.00 X 10 cans = $30 cost of ending inventory

cost of goods sold = $180

(See weighted average and first-in, first-out comparisons)

Key Point: When prices are rising LIFO results in lower income and thus a tax savings.

LEDGER

Usually transactions are first recorded into a journal and eventually posted (or information transferred) to a group of accounts called a *ledger*.

The result will eventually be a trial balance or a list of the ledger accounts.

The ledger is arranged by account numbers and is based upon the chart of accounts. In the ledger book each account is a new page.

(See accounting cycle)

Ledger

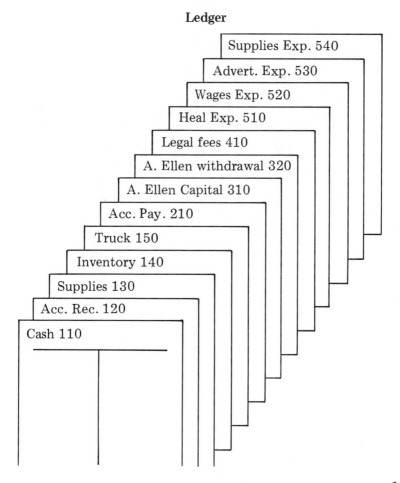

LIABILITIES (CREDITORS)

Debts or obligations owed from borrowing money for services or commodities. Liabilities represents the rights of the creditors to assets in a firm.

(See: accounts payable, promissory note, on account, current liabilities, long-term liabilities)

JOE tOOK Shelly to the MOUIES And CREATED A LIABILITY when HE Borrowed FROM Shelly TEN DOLLARS For his DATE with ANN the NEXT NIGHT

LIMITED LIABILITY

The corporation is responsible for its debts and obligations.

(For comparison see unlimited liability)

Limited Liability

Jim's Sporting Goods (a corporation) opened for business on Jan. 1, 197X.

On June 1, 198X Jim's sporting goods faced heavy losses and was forced to declare bankruptcy.

Jim, who owned a beautiful home and car, didn't have to worry about the creditors going after him for the *company's* losses.

LIQUID ASSETS (QUICK ASSETS)

Assets that can be turned into cash quickly.

(See marketable securities)

Liquid Assets (Quick Assets)

Cash
Notes Receivable
Accounts Receivable
Marketable Securities
Interest Receivable
Rent Receivable

LIQUIDATION—PARTNERSHIP

The winding-up process of a company that is going out of business.

The winding-up process includes:

1. Selling the assets of the company
2. Paying the creditors (liabilities)
3. Giving whatever cash or assets are left to the owners of the business (this results after first paying the creditors).

(See realization-partnership)

Liquidation-Partnership

Carolyn Bergstrom Hair Stylists

Cash	$10,000	
All noncash assets	60,000	
All liabilities		$10,000
T. Duffy capital		20,000
C. Bergstrom capital		20,000
C. Peterson capital		20,000
Total	$70,000	$70,000

Sold all noncash assets for $90,000 showing a gain on realization of $30,000 ($90,000 − $60,000 = $30,000).

The following entries show the sale of the noncash assets and the rest of the liquidation process:

1.
Sale of Assets:	Debit	Credit
Cash.	90,000	
Assets		60,000
Gain on realization		30,000

1.
Division of Gain to Capital:	Debit	Credit
Gain on realization	30,000	
T. Duffy, capital.		10,000
C. Bergstrom, capital		10,000
C. Peterson, capital.		10,000

2.
Payment of Liabilities:	Debit	Credit
Liabilities.	10,000	
Cash		10,000

3.
Distribution of Cash to Capital:		
T. Duffy, capital	30,000	
C. Bergstrom, capital	30,000	
C. Peterson, capital	30,000	
Cash		90,000

After Realization		
Cash	$100,000	
All liabilities		$10,000
T. Duffy capital		30,000
C. Bergstrom capital		30,000
C. Peterson capital		30,000

(Noncash assets are off the books)

LONG-TERM INVESTMENTS (ASSETS)

Assets which are accumulated by a firm to be held on a long-term basis. These assets are not directly used in producing the revenues of the firm.

(For comparison see marketable securities)

Long-Term Investments (Assets)

A Portion of a Balance Sheet

Moll Corporation
Balance Sheet
Dec. 31, 198X

Current Assets:

Cash	. $1,000	
Accounts Receivable	. 2,000	
Inventories	. 4,000	
(At Lower of Cost (FIFO) or Market)		
Total Current Assets		$7,000

Long-Term Investments:

Investment in Mayberry Co.	. $3,000	
Total Long-Term Investments		$3,000

Plant Assets:

LONG-TERM LIABILITIES

Obligations or services that we owe that will not be due for a year or more. When they become due within a year, they become current liabilities. Example: bonds payable.

(For comparison see current liabilities)

Long-Term Liabilities

A Section of a Balance Sheet

Assets

_____
_____
_____
_____
_____

Liabilities

Current Liabilities:

Notes Payable	$5,000	
Accounts Payable	2,600	
Wages Payable	400	
Total Current Liabilities		$8,000

Long-Term Liabilities

Mortgage Payable	5,000	
Total Liabilities		$13,000

Capital (Owner Equity)

MAKER

A person or company who (in writing) definitely promises to pay to the order of someone (payee) a definite sum of money at a fixed future date.

The person or company making the promise is the *maker*.

(For comparison see payee)

Maker

$3,000	Dayton, Ohio October 2 19 8X
90 Days After Date I Promise to Pay to	
The Order of_____ Mets Electronic Co.	
Three-Thousand -- Dollars	
Payable at_____ McQuire Bank	
Value Received with Interest at_____ 6%	
No. 20 Due December 1, 198X *William E. Ford, Jr.*	
(Maker)	

MARKETABLE SECURITIES

Temporary investments made by a corporation that has some idle or extra cash on hand to buy income yielding securities (stock, bonds, etc.) which can be quickly turned back into cash when needed.

When the corporation needs the money to carry on the normal operations of the business it will sell the securities.

(See long-term investments for comparison)

Marketable Securities

A Portion of a Balance Sheet

Vac's Corporation
Balance Sheet
Dec. 31, 198X

Current assets:

Cash	$5,000	
Marketable securities, at cost	500	
(market price $600)		
Merchandise inventory	1,000	
Prepaid rent	400	
Total current assets		$6,900

MATCHING PRINCIPLE (REVENUE AND EXPENSES)

Take all the revenue (sales) *earned** in a specific period of time and subtract all expenses which have arisen, or been incurred in earning that revenue.

The result will be to match revenue earned as compared to expenses and costs involved in earning that revenue—the net result being profit or loss.

(See operating statement)

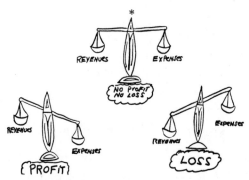

*The scales relate to height and not weight.

MATURITY DATE

The time or date when a note (a written promise to pay) becomes due.

Maturity Date

Jan. 1   Bob Singer needed a loan to buy a car.

Jan. 2   Bob borrowed $1,000 from BC Loan Company promising in writing to pay back the $1,000 plus $100 in interest on December 31 to BC Loan Company.

Dec. 31   *Maturity Date*

Bob paid BC Loan Company $1,100 ($1,000 + $100)

$1,000 = principal

$100 = interest

*Under an accrual system in accounting, a sale is recognized and recorded when it is earned whether you receive the money or not.

MERCHANDISE COMPANY

A business that sells goods or merchandise in order to earn revenue or sales.

(See cost of goods sold—merchandise company)

MERCHANDISE INVENTORY—(MERCHANDISING COMPANY)

Goods on hand in a merchandise business which are for resale to its customers.

This merchandise, or goods available to sell, is usually sold within one year to those customers.

(See LIFO, FIFO, weighted average, cost of goods sold)

MINIMUM LEGAL CAPITAL (LEGAL VALUE)

Usually it is the par or stated value of the stock that is issued by a corporation that must be kept in the business for protection of the creditors.

Each state has its own regulations for legal capital.

(See par value)

Minimum Legal Capital

Fox Corporation issued 3,000 shares of common stock ($1.00 par) to investors.

The state in which Fox operates requires that the company keep $3,000 as legal capital ($1.00 X 3,000 shares) in the business for possible protection of the creditors (since the stockholder is only liable to the amount of his investment in the company).

Key Point: When dividends are issued they cannot reduce permanent contributed capital below minimum legal capital as required by state law.

MORTGAGE NOTES PAYABLE

The amount we owe (usually a long-term debt for property) to someone (creditors). This long term liability is secured by mortgage property.

Failure on our part to pay or perform our promises, relating to the note, results in the creditor having the rights to go after certain assets (home, building, etc.).

(For comparison see notes receivable)

Direct Reduction
Mortgage Note

$18,000   Account No. __10__

                                                 December 10___   198X

I

For value received we jointly and severally, promise to pay to
                    Barbara Bresnahan
or order the sum of eighteen thousand dollars in or within 20 years from this date, with interest thereon at the rate of 8 1/2 percent per annum, payable in monthly installments of $156.21 on the first day of each month hereafter, which payments shall first be applied to interest then due and the balance thereof remaining applied to principal; the interest to be computed monthly in advance on the unpaid balance, together with such fines on interest in arrears as are provided.

With the right to make additional payments on account of said principal sum on any payment date.

Failure to pay any of said installments within thirty (30) days from the date when the same becomes due, notwithstanding any license or waiver of any prior breach of conditions, shall make the whole of the balance of said principal sum immediately due and payable at the option of the holder thereof.

The makers, endorsers, and guarantors or other parties to this note, and each of them, severally waive demand, notice and protest.

Signed and sealed in the presence of

*See promissory note.

134

NEGOTIABLE INSTRUMENT

A legal document which usually can change title (rights of ownership) quickly.

This selling or transferring is usually done by signing the document or sometimes by just delivering it.

A promissory note usually is a negotiable instrument.

(See promissory note)

Negotiable Instrument

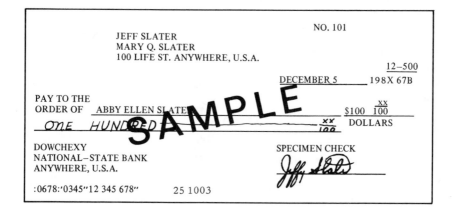

NET INCOME (NET PROFIT)

The profit or the money a business makes for specific periods of time.

Sales* (revenue) minus expenses = net income (or profit).

(See matching or operating statement)

Net Income

Bob opened up a Pizza-Bagel Deli. The first month he sold $100 worth of pizza-bagels. His expenses, or costs to produce those earned sales were $50. Bob showed a profit, or earned net income of $50 for that specific period of time.

*Earned revenue—incurred expenses. For a merchandise company see p. 110.

NET LOSS

Not making money for a specific period of time. Sales (revenue) are smaller than a company's expenses, the result being a loss.

(See matching or operating statements)

Remember: revenue minus expenses = net income.

Net Loss

Bill saw an advertisement in the local paper to invest in a super-market. It stated in the ad that last year the market made a net profit of $30,000 after all costs (expenses).

After one year in business, Bill earned sales of $500,000 but had expenses of over $600,000 (including wages, rent, advertising, sup-plies, etc.). The result being that Bill lost or showed a net loss of $100,000 for the year. Bill's wife, needless to say, has put his busi-ness up for sale.

	Sales	$500,000
—	Expenses	600,000
	Net Loss	($100,000)

Service Co.	*Merch. Co.*
Sales	Sales
— Expenses	— Cogs
	= Gross Profit
= Net Income or Net Loss	— Oper. Exp.
	= Net Income or Net Loss

NET PAY

The amount of money taken home by a worker from a business (or employer) in wages after all deductions (taxes, social security, etc.) are taken out.

(For comparison see gross pay)

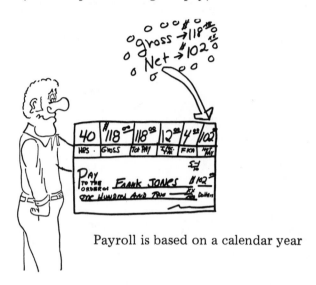

Payroll is based on a calendar year

Gross Pay
— FICA
— FWT
— SWT
— Medical
— Union
= Net Pay

NET SALES

The total revenue (cash as well as charge sales) to a business from its operation minus any sales discounts *and/or* sales returns and allowances that the business gives or issues to its customers for a specific period of time.

(See gross sales)

Net Sales

Jim's Supermarket
Income Statement
for Year Ended December 31, 198X

Revenue from sales (gross sales)		$70,000
Less: Sales discounts	$5,000	
Sales returns and allowances	3,000	8,000
Net sales		$62,000

Jim earned $70,000 from selling food to his customers; however, due to dented cans, spoilage, as well as discounts and savings given to his large customers, Jim's supermarket actually took in $62,000.

Gross sales is what he wished he took in, net earned sales is what he must be satisfied with.

(See gross sales for comparison)

NOMINAL ACCOUNTS (TEMPORARY ACCOUNTS)

All revenue, costs and expenses, drawing, as well as income summary accounts.

Balances of each account are *not carried over* to the next accounting period.

Their balances are eventually summarized in order to determine a *new figure* for capital (owner's equity) to *start* the *next* accounting period.

(See closing entries for more detail, chart at end of book)

Nominal Accounts

Sales
Sales returns and allowance
Sale discounts
Purchases
Purchase return and allowance
Purchase discount
Income summary
Withdrawals
Salary expense
Rent expense
Advertising expense
Freight-in
(any revenue, expense, cost are temporary)

NONCUMULATIVE PREFERRED STOCK

A type of stock which usually gives to the investor a definite or certain amount of dividends each year.

If, for some reason, the dividends are not paid (in arrears) that year, or in the past years, the holders of noncumulative preferred stock are *not* entitled to the past dividends when current dividends are paid.

(See cumulative preferred stock)

Noncumulative Preferred Stock

Barry Katz bought 100 shares of noncumulative preferred stock of Moore Corporation through his local home town stockbroker.

The stockbroker had told Barry that this type of stock *will pay* him a $100 dividend per year.

However, if the company, for some reason, cannot pay a dividend (is in arrears), Barry *will not have rights* to the past unpaid dividends when present or future dividends are paid.

(See cumulative preferred stock for comparison)

NONPARTICIPATING PREFERRED STOCK

A type of stock which usually gives to the investor a definite or fixed amount of dividends from the corporation.

There is no opportunity for the preferred stockholders to "participate" or share in more or additional dividends that year.

Most preferred stock is nonparticipating.

(See cumulative preferred stock for further help)

Nonparticipating Preferred Stock

Facts: (Relating to Bobreck Company)

1. There are 1,000 shares of preferred nonparticipating stock outstanding.

2. There are 5,000 shares of common stock outstanding (issued).

3. Holders of preferred stock get $1.00 per share each year (not allowed to join with common stockholders if more dividends are available).

4. Common stockholders get what is left after paying off the preferred stockholders.

Situation: A look at Bobreck for 198X and 199X relating to dividends.

	198X	198X Dividend Share	199X	199X Dividend Share
Total dividends* to be paid	$1,000		$11,000	
To preferred	$1,000 (1,000 shr. X $1.00)	$1.00 $1,000 / 1,000 shrs.	$ 1,000 (1,000 shrs. X $1.00)	$1.00 ($1,000) / 1,000 shr.
To common	0	0	$10,000 (5,000 shrs. X $2.00)	$2.00 ($10,000) / 5,000 shr.

*based on company earnings

(See cumulative preferred for other possibilities)

141

NORMAL BALANCE—ACCOUNT

The usual balance that an account will have after all the increases and decreases (debits and credits) have been summarized.

Normal Balance

	Normal Balance
assets	debit
liabilities	credit
capital (owners' equity)	credit
drawing	debit
expenses	debit
revenue	credit
retained earnings	credit
(for specific titles see foldout chart at end of book)	

If cash (an asset) has a credit balance, what would it mean? We have overdrawn our checkbook, because we have a negative balance in cash. This situation would not be the normal balance of cash.

NOTES PAYABLE

The amount we owe someone (creditors). Because we have made a definite written promise which states that we will pay to the order of someone (payee) a certain amount of money at a certain date. Notes payable is a liability on the balance sheet.

(For opposite side of coin, see notes receivable)

Notes Payable

When Moe decided to buy a car, he had to sign a note stipulating that each month he would pay $100 plus interest for 30 months. Formal papers were drawn up and Moe had created a liability, or notes payable, which meant he now owed a set amount of money to pay to the car dealer for a fixed period of time in the future.

NOTES RECEIVABLE

Someone owes us money and we have a written promise which states when we will receive a certain amount of money by a given date in the future. Notes receivable is an asset in the balance sheet.

(See accounts receivable for comparison/or notes payable)

ON ACCOUNT

To charge it. Buy now, pay later!

(See accounts payable)

ORGANIZATION COSTS

The cost or expenditure which results from organizing a new company.

The total of all the costs are considered to be an *intangible* asset called organization costs.

Organization Costs

January 5: Enid Silberstein spent $1,000 for printing up stock certificates, paying legal fees, as well as paying the cost of getting a state charter in order to form Messer Corporation. The following entry was recorded by Messer Corporation:

Journal   Page #1

Date		Description (Accounts)	Folio (PR)	Debit	Credit
198X Jan.	5	Organization cost	10	1,000	
		Cash	1		1,000

At the end of the first year, a portion of the balance sheet of Meser Corporation looked as follows:

Assets:

Current Assets:

_____

_____

_____

Plant Assets:

_____

_____

_____

Intangible Assets:

Organization costs $1,000

Goodwill   500

Total Assets:

OUTSTANDING CHECKS (CHECKS IN TRANSIT)

Checks written by a person or company that have not been received, or processed (or cleared) by the bank.

This would be subtracted from the bank balance in the preparation of a bank reconciliation.

(See bank reconciliation)

PAID-IN CAPITAL (CONTRIBUTED CAPITAL)

A section of stockholders' equity which shows:

1. Amount of stock a corporation has issued (or sold)
2. The premiums or discounts that have resulted from selling stock
3. The sale of treasury stock*
4. Stock received from donations

Stockholders' Equity = Paid-in capital + retained earnings
(Contributed capital)

Paid-in Capital (Contributed Capital)

Stockholders' Equity (stockholders' investment)

Paid-in capital:		
(contributed capital)		
Common stock	$400,000	
($10 par, 40,000 shares issued)		
Premimum on common stock	80,000	$480,000
(stock was sold at $12 per share or		
a $2 premium per share)		
From sale of treasury stock		10,000
Total paid-in capital (contributed)		$490,000

*See treasury stock.

145

PAR VALUE

A dollar value which is assigned to a share of stock arbitrarily (or at random).

Each state has its own regulations whether a corporation needs to assign a par value or not.

Why use par?

Par value is sometimes used to protect the creditors.

Some state laws require a corporation to keep a certain amount of the stockholders' investment in the business for the protection of the creditors. (This is called legal capital.)

Par value may be used in calculating legal capital.

(See minimum legal capital)

Courtesy of E.F. Hutton.

146

PARTICIPATING PREFERRED STOCK

A type of stock which usually gives to the investor a definite or certain amount of dividends (from the corporation) each year with the opportunity of the preferred stockholder to "participate" or share in more or additional dividends.

(See cumulative preferred stock for further help)

Participating Preferred Stock

Facts: (Relating to Bobreck Company)
1. There are 1,000 shares of preferred (participating) stock outstanding (issued).
2. There are 5,000 shares of common stock outstanding.
3. Holders of preferred stock get at least $1.00 per share each year.
4. Common stockholders get up to $1.00 per share before having to split with preferred (see No. 5).
5. Whatever is left (after common and preferred have been paid) or available to be paid out in dividends is split one-sixth to preferred and five-sixths to common (these are the rules of Bobreck).

Situation: A look at Bobreck for 197X and 198X relating to dividends:

	197X	197X Dividend Share	198X	
Total dividends* to be paid	$1,000		$12,000	
To preferred	$1,000 (1,000 shrs. X $1.00)	$1.00 $1,000 / 1,000 shr.	$ 2,000 $1,000 + 1,000 (1/6 X $6,000)	$2.00 $2,000 / 1,000 shrs.
To common	0	0	$10,000 $5,000 + 5,000 (5/6 X $6,000)	$2.00 $10,000 / 5,000 shrs.

*Based on company's earnings

(See cumulative preferred for other possibilities)

PARTNERSHIP

A business owned by *two or more* people. (How the ownership is divided should be spelled out in a legal contract to avoid disputes later on.)

(See liquidation, or realization)

Partnership

Characteristics: Unlimited liability
Ease of formation
Limited life

PATENTS (INTANGIBLE ASSETS)

An exclusive right for 17 years, which is granted by the federal government which allows one to sell, use, or manufacture a certain type of product.

Patents

Morris Blue, a retired shoe worker, invented a new type of car which uses air for fuel instead of gas.

Morris applied for a patent with the federal government. If granted Morris would have the exclusive right to manufacture the car.

PAYABLE

Means to owe. It is a liability. A payable account is a liability.

(See on account)

Payable

Jim bought a television from Cotoia, Inc.

He charged it for $100. Cotoia called Jim an accounts receivable, and Jim called Cotoia, Inc. an accounts payable (or he owed Cotoia, Inc. money).

PAYEE (PROMISSORY NOTE)

The person or company who will *receive* money (check) from a promissory note (a definite written promise to pay us [*payee*] a definite sum of money at a fixed future date). The person or company making this promise is the maker.

(See note receivable for further help)

(See maker for comparison)

PAYEE

$3,000	DAYTON, OHIO	OCTOBER 2 198X

90 DAYS _____ AFTER DATE ____ I _____ PROMISE TO PAY TO
THE ORDER OF _____ METS ELECTRONIC CO.

_____ THREE - THOUSAND ------------------------------ DOLLARS

PAYABLE AT _____ McQUIRE BANK

VALUE RECEIVED WITH INTEREST AT ____ 6% ____

NO. ____ 20 ____ DUE DECEMBER 1, 198X   *Nancy Ford*

PAYEE

PAYROLL

The total amount of wages or salaries which are paid to workers of a business for a specific period of time.*

*Payroll is based on a calendar year for tax purposes.

(See payroll register, net pay, gross pay, FICA)

Payroll is based upon a calendar year which is broken into four quarters.

Quarter 1	Quarter 2	Quarter 3	Quarter 4
January	April	July	October
February	May	August	November
March	June	September	December

PAYROLL REGISTER

A form (many columns) which contains and summarizes information about payroll (amount of money paid to workers less deductions) which is needed at the end of each payroll period.*

The payroll register may be used as a supplementary record or as a special journal.

(See employer's payroll taxes)

Payroll Register

Payroll Register   Week Ended January 8, 198X

Employees (workers)	Time Clock Card No.	Daily Time M T W T F S S	Tot. Hrs.	O.T. Hrs.	Reg. Pay Rate	Earnings		
						Reg. Pay Befr.	O.T. Prem. Pay	Gross Pay
Jim Snively	15	8 8 8 8 8 8 8	40		$2.50	$100		$100
Carl Bartlet	6	8 8 8 6 0 0 0	30		2.00	60		60
Pat Elario	3	8 8 8 8 8 0 0	40		2.50	100		100
John Riley	1	8 8 8 8 8 4 0	44	4	3.00	120	$18.00	138
						$380	$18.00	$398

Deductions					Payments	
F.I.C.A. Taxes	Federal Income Taxes	Medical Insurance	Labor Union Dues	Total Deductions	Net Pay (take home)	Check Number
$ 5.00	$ 7.00	$ 2.50	$ 4.00	$18.50	$ 81.50	103
3.00	5.20	4.00	2.50	14.70	45.30	104
5.00	9.10	4.00	2.50	20.60	79.40	105
6.90	10.70	4.00	2.50	24.10	113.90	106
19.90	32.00	14.50	11.50	77.90	320.10	

*Payroll is based on a calendar year for tax purposes.

PENCIL FOOTING

Summarizing the debits (left side of any account) and credits (right side of any account) of an account to get a new balance.

Pencil Footing

Cash

100	200
200	50
500	60
800	*310*
490	

The side which has the largest amount of balance ($800) is not moved while the smaller side ($310) is brought over and subtracted. The new balance ($490) remains on the side which had the largest amount or balance.

PERIODIC INVENTORY SYSTEM

An inventory system which does not try at the time of each sale of merchandise (good) to calculate the *cost* of each "good" that is sold by the company.

In this system one waits until the end of an accounting period to determine at one time the *cost of all goods (merchandise) sold* by the company during this period.

(See perpetual inventory for comparison)

(For calculating a cost of ending inventory, see FIFO, LIFO, weighted average, gross profit method and retail method)

It is merchandise inventory account which show the beginning inventory. It is the purchase account which records the cost of additional purchases. At end of period a physical count of inventory is taken to determine the cost of goods sold.

PERPETUAL INVENTORY SYSTEM

An inventory system which keeps *continual* track of how much inventory (merchandise, goods) is on hand.

This system usually uses forms (cards) that keep track of the number or amount of each good received or sold.

Usually once a year physical count is taken to verify the records.

(See periodic inventory for comparison)

INVENTORY CONTROL

Part No. __141__

Description __Ball Bearing__   Maximum __30__

Prime Supplier __Machinery Company__   Reorder Level __10__

Location __Warehouse (Bin 44)__   Reorder Quantity __20__

Date	Received			Sold			Balance		
	Units	Cost/Unit	Total	Units	Cost/Unit	Total	Units	Cost/Unit	Total
19XX July 1	Balance Fwd.						8	$60	$240
4	20	64	$680				8	60	
							20	64	880
				8	$60	$240			
7				8	64	256	12	64	384

Key Points:

1. Balance of inventory account continuallly updated.
2. At time of sale cogs is recorded.
3. A purchase account is not used.

PETTY CASH FUND

A sum of money that is set aside (in a fund) that allows a company to pay *cash* for its small bills or obligations instead of having to write a check (this is usually done with vouchers).

(See example of illustrating a voucher)

Petty Cash Voucher

	Voucher Number	658
	Date	5/31/8X

Paid to __Gants__

Purpose __supplies__

(Attach supporting documents below)

Gants		Balance carried forward	$31.83
Nov-2 8 1 3		This expenditure	.77
$ 0.25GrA		Balance	31.06
$ 0.25GrA		Amount replenished	18.94
$ 0.25GrA		Balance	$50.00
$ 0.02TxA			
*$ 0.77TlA			

Use only when replenishment is made.

*Most petty cash vouchers show only specific payments with no running balance.

The establishment of petty cash results in a debit to petty cash and a credit to cash.

The payments out of petty cash are recorded in the auxiliary petty cash record—it is at time of replenishment that the individual expenses will be debted and a cover check written to replenish petty cash.

The only time petty cash is debited would be to raise it to a new level.

155

POST-CLOSING TRIAL BALANCE (POST-CLEARING TRIAL BALANCE)

A trial balance (list of the ledger) which is taken *after* the adjusting and closing entries have been posted to the ledger.

The post-closing trial balance should contain *only* permanent accounts (assets, liabilities, and one new figure for capital). All temporary accounts (revenue, expense, drawing, as well as income summary) have *zero* balances. *They do not appear on the post-closing trial balance.*

Once again, the post-closing trial balance shows equality of debits and credits in the ledger.

Joe's Market
Post-Closing Trial Balance
for Year Ended December 31, 198X

	Debit	Credit
Cash	1,000	
Accounts receivable	500	
Merchandise inventory	200	
Equipment	100	
Accumulated depreciation-equipment		50
Accounts payable		450
J. Smith, capital		1,300
	1,800	1,800

Key Point: By journalizing and posting the closing entries to the ledger all temporary accounts have a zero balance and this information has been summarized in J. Smith, capital.

POST-REFERENCE (FOLIO) (ACCOUNT NUMBER)

A. In a journal, a column which shows the number of the account to which information has been transferred (posted) to the ledger.

B. In a ledger it is a column which shows the number of the journal page from which a posting or transfer of information has come.

Post-Reference (Folio)

General Journal   Page #5

Date		Description	Folio (PR)	Debit	Credit
198X Nov.	1	Cash	12	500	
		Sales	4		500
		(Cash sales for the day)			

Ledger

Cash   Account No. 12

Date	Explanation	Folio (PR)	Debit	Date	Explanation	Folio (PR)	Credit
198X Nov. 1		GJ 5	$500				

Sales   Account No. 4

Date	Explanation	Folio (PR)	Debit	Date	Explanation	Folio (PR)	Credit
				198X Nov. 1		GJ5	500

Key Point: PR numbers should never be recorded until posting is finished. One purpose of PR numbers is to indicate whether or not posting has been completed.

PREEMPTIVE RIGHT

The stockholders in a corporation have the right to buy *additional* (or more) shares of stock when the corporation sells new shares of stock.

The stockholder would buy more stock *in order to keep his same fractional amount* (or proportional) *interest* or *rights* in the corporation.

Preemptive Right

Jim Tabbut owns 25% of all the common stock issued by AV Laboratories.

On January 5, AV Laboratories announced an intent to sell an additional 100,000 new shares of common stock.

Jim called the company because he was concerned about losing his 25% interest in the company.

The company assured Jim that under preemptive rights he would be given the option to buy 25,000 shares of the new issue if he wanted, although he surely would not be forced into buying the new stock.

PREFERRED STOCK

To the investor:

A type of stock which shows the amount of ownership and rights one has in a corporation.

This type of stock usually gives the investor certain special priviledged rights to how they may share in the profits or earnings of a corporation during the year.

To a corporation:

This usually means a way of raising money (from a wider variety of investors) by selling shares of preferred stock to investors.

Some investors who do not like common stock *may* invest in preferred stock.

(See common stock)

FULL PAID AND NON-ASSESSABLE

Common Stock, 2,000 Shares without Par Value
Preferred Stock, $500,000, Shares $10 Each

BETHLEHEM KID COMPAI

INCORPORATED UNDER THE LAWS OF THE STATE OF DELAWARE

ABBEY ELLEN SLATER

THIS IS TO CERTIFY that

owner of _____ *Seventy Five* Shares of the PREFERRED Stock of the par BETHLEHEM KID COMPANY, *transferable on the books of the Corporation by the holder hereof in person or by duly upon surrender of this Certificate properly endorsed.*

The Preferred Stock may be issued as and when the Board of Directors shall determine and shall entitle the holder of the net earnings; and the Corporation shall be bound to pay a fixed cumulative dividend at the rate of but not exceedi per annum, payable annually on the first day of March in each year, before any dividend shall be set apart or paid or

After a dividend of seven per centum, together with all accumulated dividends, has been set apart or paid on the any one year, and Seven Dollars per share has been set apart or paid as a dividend on the Common Stock during sai earnings to be distributed as dividends during said year shall be distributed one-half in amount to the holders of the one-half in amount to the holders of the Common Stock.

At all meetings of stockholders for election of Directors, the holders of the Common Stock shall be entitled to el of the Board of Directors, and the holders of the Preferred Stock shall be entitled to elect the balance of the Board of I

In the event of liquidation or dissolution of the Corporation, the holders of the Preferred Stock shall be entitled to par and accumulated dividends before any amount shall be paid to the holders of the Common Stock, and after the ho Stock shall have been paid in full as to par and accumulated dividends, and the hol Stock shall have been paid an amount equal to $100 per share, then any remaining asse one-half to the holders of the Preferred Stock and one-half to the holders of the Com WITNESS the seal of the Corporation and the signatures of its duly auth

Courtesy of E.F. Hutton.

159

PREMIUM ON STOCK (CAPITAL CONTRIBUTED
IN EXCESS OF PAR)

The result of selling stock (or issuing stock) at a price that is *greater* than par value.

(See par value for further help, discount on stock)

Premium On Stock

On July 1, the Blance Corporation issued 500 shares, $10 par common stock at $12 per share.

The following entry was made on the company's books:

Journal   Page #1

Date		Description (Accounts)	Folio (PR)	Debit	Credit
198X July	1	Cash	1	6,000	
		Common stock	10		5,000*
		Premium on common stock	11		1,000

*(500 shares x $10 par)

(See discount on stock for comparison)

Key Point: Premium on common stock is a capital account on the corporate balance sheet with a normal balance of a credit.

PREPAID EXPENSES

Expenses that have been paid for ahead of time. When you get them, they are assets, when you use them up they become expenses. Prepaid expenses are located on the balance sheet with a debit balance.

Prepaid Expenses

Ed Sloan opened up a dress shop, but his landlord, not trusting him, demanded Ed pay three months rent in advance.

The transaction was recorded as follows:

Journal   Page #1

Date		Description (Accounts)	Folio (PR)	Debit	Credit
198X Jan.	1	Prepaid rent	5	XXXX	
		Cash	1		XXXX

PREPAID RENT

Paying ahead of time for rent which has not been used up yet. When it gets used up it will be an expense, but for now it is an asset (property or thing of value owned by the business).

Prepaid Rent

John Mills paid 3 months rent $900 in advance to Mills Real Estate. At end of 1st year the asset prepaid rent now had a balance of $600 since $300 was now recorded as rent expense.

PRINCIPLE OF CONSERVATISM

A guideline or rule which, in the past, tended to emphasize that a company should not be too optimistic in valuing certain accounts, but should take a more conservative view (which would reduce net income or lessen an asset's value).

This principle looked ahead to the possibilities of a company not having profit and therefore, having to provide for its losses (a very conservative attitude).

The attitude toward this principle is changing and concepts of materiality, objectivity and consistency, etc., are being considered before the principle of conservatism, although conservatism is still a consideration.

CONSERVATIVE   MODERN

PRINCIPLE OF CONSISTENCY

A business may use many different accounting rules or guidelines to prepare their income and balance sheet statements in an attempt to reflect fairly net income.

In order for a person to compare a company's statements from year to year (to see trends or how a company is doing) one must be sure the company is using the same accounting principles (or is being consistent) each year to prepare those statements.

Principle of Consistency

With inflation, Jones Corporation changed from FIFO to LIFO, the result being less profit and also paying less taxes. The editor of a local paper questions why the principle of consistency was being followed in the best interest of the public.

162

PRINCIPLE OF MATERIALITY

Instances when a business doesn't have to strictly follow certain accounting principles when:

1. The cost of implementing that principle is excessive (or prohibitive) to follow, and

2. The business financial statement will *not* be greatly effected.

To decide about materiality is often a "judgement decision."

Principle of Materiality

James Corporation bought a desk lamp for two dollars.

The company felt that they should record the cost of the lamp as an expense (instead of an asset) because it would cost more to depreciate it over five years (to the company) and the result of recording it as an expense would not materially effect the outcome of James' financial statements.

PRINCIPLE OF OBJECTIVITY

When a business performs the accounting cycle (recording transactions, preparing statements, etc.) it must be able to back up (or verify) factually the figures or data that have been used.

This is done by a company keeping copies of its records (bills, bank statements, purchase orders, etc.).

If records are not available, a company may have to show the logic or sound judgement that was used (maybe how an estimate for bad debts was made) to arrive at a certain figure.

PRIVATE ACCOUNTANT

A worker (employee) who is doing accounting for a company. He works only for that company.

(See public accountant)

Private Accountant

Francis Manning opened up a hot dog and milk stand. The operation became so big that Frank hired a full-time person to handle the accounting.

PROMISSORY NOTE

A promise in writing to pay a definite amount of money at a certain date (as agreed upon in the agreement) signed by the *maker.*

(See maker for detail, mortgage note payable)

MERCHANTS-WARREN NATIONAL BANK
of SALEM

...., 19
City   State

For value received, the undersigned maker(s), jointly and severally, promise to pay to the order of Merchants-Warren National Bank of Salem
place.. dollars ($........................)
..........consecutive monthly payments of $.............. each, except the final installment which shall be the balance then due. The first installm
....and the remaining installments to be paid on the..............day of each subsequent month until paid in full,
interest at the rate of 5% on each installment after maturity. Any unpaid balance may be paid, at any time, without penalty and any unearned f
will be refunded based on the "Rule of 78's". Whenever any installment shall not be paid within fifteen (15) days of its due date, the undersigne
addition thereto, a late charge in the amount of 5% of the overdue payment or $5.00, whichever is less.
There has been deposited with said Bank as collateral security for the payment of this and all other liabilities of the undersigned to the l
whether now or hereafter incurred, absolute or contingent, direct or indirect, due or to become due or that may be hereafter contracted, the
scribed property (if none, so state):..
....

Any and all deposits or other sums at any time or times credited by or due from the holder to, and all securities or other property in pos
holder for safekeeping or otherwise and belonging to, any maker, indorser, or guarantor of this note are and shall be subject to a security interest i
holder to secure payment of this note and the payment and performance of any and all other liabilities and obligations, direct or indirect, absolute
due or to become due or that may hereafter be contracted, of said respective maker, indorser, or guarantor to the holder. Upon any of the events s
or upon non-payment of this note or of any such liability whenever due, and at any time or times thereafter, without any demand or notice, exce
tent as notice may be required by applicable law, the holder may sell or dispose of any or all of such securities or other property and may exercise
the rights accorded the holder by the Massachusetts Uniform Commercial Code. The holder may apply or set off such deposits or other sums at a
case of deposits of, or other sums due to, makers of this note, but only with respect to matured liabilities in the case of indorsers or guarantors of
provisions of this paragraph are cumulative to, and not exclusive of, any other rights that the holder has with respect to such deposits, sums, secu
property under other agreements or applicable principles of law. The holder shall have no duty to take steps to preserve rights against prior part
securities or other property.
In case of the failure of the undersigned to pay any installment on its due date, or if a petition under the Bankruptcy Act shall be filed by
of the undersigned or any endorser or guarantor, or if any of the undersigned or any endorser or guarantor shall die or make a general assignment f
of creditors or shall have property attached by any legal or equitable process, the entire unpaid balance of this note, less any unearned interest
"Rule of 78's", shall at the option of the holder, become forthwith due and payable. The undersigned (jointly and severally if more than one) a
expenses of Collection including reasonable attorney's fees.

Courtesy of Merchants Warren National Bank.

PROTEST NOTICE

A written statement by a bank which tells of the failure of someone (the maker) to pay his note or written promise when it came due (maturity).

This statement is sent to the person who is contingently liable (now responsible to pay for the note or promise to the bank because the other person [maker] failed to pay).

(See contingent liability for more detail)

Protest Notice

On June 2, the Blue Bank notified Jim Driscoll that he must pay a note receivable that was dishonored by Joe Walker. Why?

This is the way it happened:

On January 1, Joe Walker promised in writing to pay Jim Driscoll a $100 note on June 1.

On January 2, Jim Driscoll decided he couldn't wait for the money and discounted the note at the Blue Bank, with a stipulation that, if Joe Walker didn't pay off his promise on June 1, he would pay it to the bank (Jim being contingently liable).

Well, on June 1, Joe Walker never paid so the bank sent a *protest notice* to Jim Driscoll.

PUBLIC ACCOUNTANT

A person who provides an accounting service (or function) to the general public for a certain fee.

(See private accountant)

Public Accountant

Ed Monroe just opened up a small health lounge. He really didn't understand how to set up an accounting system; therefore, he called in a public accounting firm to act as consultants. Ed's business *never* grew so big that it *required* a full-time accountant.

PUNCH CARD

Input ↴

A card or document that has holes punched in it to represent letters or numbers, etc., which can be "placed" or "fed" into the computer in order to process information.

Output ↴

A punch card can also contain information that has been processed by the computer.

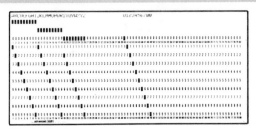

PURCHASE ACCOUNT

An account which shows or accumulates the amount of merchandise (goods) bought or purchased for resale to one's customers.

Purchase has a debit balance and is also found on the income statement.

(See purchase discount/or purchase, returns and allowances)

Purchase Account

On January 4, The B and L Supermarket bought $5,000 worth of merchandise (goods or purchases for resale to its customers) on account from Keeney Food Wholesalers.

The B and L Supermarket made the following transaction to record the purchase: ↴

Journal   Page #1

Date		Description (Accounts)	Folio (PR)	Debit	Credit
198X Jan.	4	Purchases	5	5,000	
		Accounts payable—	8		5,000
		Keeney Food Wholesaler			

(See cost of goods sold for more information)

PURCHASE DISCOUNT ACCOUNT

An account which shows the savings or reduction of costs by a company that pays for merchandise before a discount date set by the seller. Purchase discount balance found on the income statement has a credit balance.

(See purchase account, purchase returns and allowances)

Purchase Discount

Jan. 5 Moe Glass Inc. bought $300 worth of purchases (merchandise for resale) from Jim's wholesale lobster company. Terms of sale were 2/10, N/30 (if Moe paid the bill within 10 days, he receives 2% or $6 off the bill). The following entry was recorded:

	Journal			Page #1	
Date	Description (accounts)	Folio (PR)	Debit	Credit	
198X Jan. 5	Purchases	10	300		
	Accounts payable—Jim's	12		300	

Jan. 8 Moe Glass pays the bill. The following entry was recorded:

	Journal			Page #2	
Date	Description (accounts)	Folio (PR)	Debit	Credit	
198X Jan. 8	Accounts payable	12	300		
	Purchase discount	11		6	
	Cash	1		294	

(See sales discount for comparison)

Key Point: Purchase discount is a temporary account.

PURCHASE JOURNAL

A book or place (special journal) where transactions are recorded when buying something (purchase, supplies, etc.) *on account* (buy now, pay later).

Purchase Journal

Transactions:

Dec. 3 Bought merchandise on account from J.P. Shoes $3,000.

Dec. 5 Bought store supplies on account, $200, from V-Supplies.

Dec. 8 Bought a car on account, $5,000, from T.T. Used Cars.

Purchase Journal

Date 198X		Accounts Credited	Folio (PR)	Accounts Payable Credit	Purchase Debit	Store Supplies Debit	Account Fol. Am't (PR)		
Dec.	3	J.P. shoes	√	3,000	3,000				
	5	V-supplies	√	200		200			
	8	T.T. used crs.	√	5,000			equip.	215	5,000
		Total		8,200		200			5,000
				(211)	(510)	(281)			√

Accounts Payable

During the month post to J.P. Shoes, V-Supplies, and T.T. Used Cars in the A/P subsidiary ledger as credits. When this is done, checks (√) are placed in the post reference column.

The total ($8,200) is posted too, as a credit to A/P account #211 in the general ledger at the end of the month.

Purchases

The total of the column is posted at *the end of the month* to purchases account number 510 in the general ledger.

Store Supplies

The total of this column is posted at *the end of the month* to store supplies account #281 in the general ledger.

The total of this column is never posted. A check (√) is placed to show this.

A debit to equipment (account #215) is posted to the general ledger *any time during the month.*

PURCHASE ORDER

A form used by the purchasing department to order some goods or merchandise.

Purchase Order

7451174	End, Inc. P.O. Box 10 26 Sable Road Salem, Ma 01945

P.O. Number

This number must appear on all shipping labels, invoice packing slips and B/L.

SHIP TO:

TO:

Date of Order	Date Needed	Ship Via	FOB
Terms	For Resale	For Own Use	Dept. or Req. No.	Ac't #
Quotation No.				

Quantity		Please Supply Items Listed Below	Price	Amount
Ordered	Received			

In consideration of end entering into this agreement with __vendor__ , __vendor__ warrants that all goods sold hereunder shall not contain hazardous substances, as defined under the provisions of the federal hazardous substances act and the regulations issued thereunder, and __vendor__ agrees to indemnify and hold harmless from any breach of this warranty.

Authorized by _____

169

PURCHASES RETURNS AND ALLOWANCES ACCOUNT

An account which shows the amount of merchandise (goods) returned to suppliers for a price reduction allowed by suppliers for defective or returned goods.

Purchases returns and allowances have a credit balance (or reduce the cost of purchases). Purchase returns and allowances is a temporary account found on the income statement.

(See purchase discounts)

Purchases Returns, and Allowances

On Jan. 5, Moe Glass Inc. bought $300 worth of lobsters (purchases for resale) on account from Jim's Wholesale Lobster Company.

On Jan. 6, Moe Glass issued a debit memo (reducing what they owed Jim's Wholesale) and returned $100 worth of lobsters to Jim's Wholesale because these lobsters were diseased.

Moe made the following entry:

Journal   Page #1

Date		Description (accounts)	Folio (PR)	Debit	Credit
198X Jan.	6	Accounts payable— Jim's whls. lobs.	10	100	
		Purchases returns and allow.	12		100

QUICK ASSETS (LIQUID ASSETS)

Something (asset) a business owns that is very close to being considered as good as cash (if that asset has to be turned into cash) for some need of the business.

Quick Assets (Liquid Assets)

Cash
Notes Receivable

Accounts Receivable
Marketable Securities

RATE OF RETURN ON ASSETS

Net income (profit divided by total assets* [current and long-term]) which give us an indication of how profitable the business was compared to the amount of assets invested in the business.

Rate of return on assets helps to answer the question of how efficiently did the company use its assets.

Rate of Return on Assets

1.	Net income after taxes	19,000
2.	Add interest costs	1,000
3.	Net income before interest costs	20,000
4.	Total assets at start of the year	400,000
5.	Total assets at end of the year	500,000
6.	Average of assets used	450,000

$$\text{Rate of return on assets used} = \frac{\text{Line 3}}{\text{Line 6}} = \frac{\$20,000}{450,000} = 4.4\%$$

Is it good or bad?

One must check previous years' ratios of the company as well as ratios of other companies in the same type of industry in order to come up with some type of meaningful analysis.

*See example if you want to use average total of assets.

RATE OF RETURN ON STOCKHOLDER'S EQUITY

Net income (profit) divided by stockholder's equity.*
This measures how productive the owner's equity was.

Rate of Return on Stockholder's Equity

1.	Net income after taxes	$100,000
2.	Common stockholders' equity, start of year	200,000
3.	Common stockholders' equity, end of year	300,000
4.	Average common stockholders' equity	250,000

Rate of return on common stockholders' equity:

$$\frac{(\text{Line 1})}{(\text{Line 4})} \quad \frac{\$100,000}{250,000} = 40\%$$

One must check previous years' ratios of the company as well as ratios of other companies in the same type of industry, in order to come up with some type of meaningful analysis.

REAL ACCOUNTS (PERMANENT)

Assets, liabilities, and capital (owner's equity). Each ending balance is carried over to the next accounting period.

(See nominal accounts)

Real Accounts (Permanent)

Assets	Liabilities	Capital
Cash	Accounts payable	Capital (owners equity)
Supplies	Notes payable	Retained earnings
Prepaid rent	Mortgage payable	
Equipment	Dividends payable	

Temporary Accounts

All revenues, expenses, income summary and drawing.

*(See example of how to get an average of stockholder's equity.)

REALIZATION—PARTNERSHIP

The amount of money that is received (or realized) in *selling assets* during the "winding up process" by a company that is going out of business.

(See liquidation)

Carolyn Bergstrom Hair Stylists

Before Liquidation

Cash	$10,000	
All noncash assets	60,000	
All liabilities		$10,000
T. Duffy, capital		20,000
C. Bergstrom, capital		20,000
C. Peretson, capital		20,000
Total	$70,000	$70,000

Sold all noncash assets for $90,000 showing a gain in realization of $30,000.

The entries to record the several steps in the liquidation process as follows:

		Journal		Page #1	

Date		Description (accounts)	Folio (PR)	Debit	Credit
198X Jan.	1	Cash		90,000	
		Assets			60,000
		Gain on realization			30,000

		Journal		Page #1	

Date		Description (accounts)	Folio (PR)	Debit	Credit
198X Jan.	1	Gain on realization		30,000	
		T. Duffy, capital			10,000
		C. Bergstrom, capital			10,000
		C. Peterson, capital			10,000

173

After Realization

Cash	$100,000	
All liabilities		$ 10,000
T. Duffy, capital		30,000
C. Bergstrom, capital		30,000
C. Peterson, capital		30,000
Total	$100,000	$100,000

(All noncash assets off books)

REGISTERED BONDS

The company issuing registered bonds keeps an *up to date* record of the names and addresses or each bond holder.

The bond can be transferred from one to another, therefore, the company keeps track of the bond owner (or new owners) which results in *less problems of theft or loss.*

Payments of interest are then sent to the owner of *record.*

Registered Bonds

John Driscoll, owner of a registered bond, transferred ownership of his bond to Pete Williams (by signing over the bond).

Pete Williams failed to notify the company and the interest payment by the company was sent to John Driscoll. Needless to say, adjustments were made to transfer the interest payments to Pete, as well as officially get Pete Williams' name on the records of the company (for payments in the future).

RESIDUAL VALUE

A *portion of the cost* of a plant asset (equipment) that one expects to get back when it is removed or has reached the end of its productive life.

Residual value is hard to estimate but gives us an estimate of how much depreciation should be taken of a plant asset (equipment) over its lifetime.

Equipment — residual value = amount of depreciation to be taken over the lifetime of a plant asset.

Residual Value

Warren Ford bought a new truck for his sales fleet for $5,000.

Based on guidelines set up by the Internal Revenue, as well as past history of his other vehicles, Warren estimated in five years he could sell or trade the truck in the market place for $200.

Warren calculated he would depreciate the truck $4,800 over the next 5 years.

Truck	—	residual value	=	amount to be depreciated
$5,000		$200		$4,800

RETAIL METHOD INVENTORY

A method used by a retail business to assign a cost or dollar figure for *ending* inventory at the end of a period of time (month, three months, etc.) and thus estimate cost of goods sold.

This method saves the business from having to physically count ending inventory *each time* an income statement is wanted by management. A physical count of inventory should be done for the end of the year statements.

Retail Method Inventory

	Cost to Store	(Price to Customers) Retail Price
Beginning merchandise inventory	$10,000	$20,000
Net purchases (less returns etc.)	30,000	60,000
Cost of merchandise available to sell to the customers (at cost and retail)	$40,000	$80,000

$$\frac{\text{Cost}}{\text{Retail}} \quad \frac{\$40,000}{\$80,000} = 50\%$$

If sales for January 1 (net) =	$50,000
and ending inventory on January 31 at retail =	30,000
The cost of ending inventory on January 31 at cost =	15,000

(50% x $30,000)

Steps:

1. Calculate cost to retail %.
2. Estimate the ending inventory at retail by deducting sales from the merchandise available for sale at retail.
3. Reduce the inventory at retail to cost.

RETAINED EARNINGS

That portion or part of profits (or earnings) of a corporation
that are kept or retained in the business which have been accumulating or building up in the business over the years.

If a corporation has a deficit (or loses money) it would reduce
retained earnings.

The amount of retained earnings doesn't mean how much cash
the business has.

(See deficit—retained earnings)

Retained Earnings
Stockholders' Equity (Shareholders' Equity)

Paid-In Captial:
(Contributed Capital)

Common Stock	$100,000	Ret. Earnings	(Jan. 1) $10,000
Retained Earnings	20,000 ——▶ + Net Income	(Jan.) $10,000
	= Ret. Earnings	(Jan. 31) $20,000
Total Stockholders' Equity	$120,000		

RETAINED EARNINGS STATEMENT

A report or statement which shows the *changes that have taken
place* in retained earnings during an accounting period.

Retained Earnings Statement

Metzner Co.
Retained Earnings Statement
for Year Ended December 31, 198X

Retained Earnings, Jan. 1, 198X		$10,000
Add: Net income per income statement	$6,000	
Collection of income tax refund	3,500	9,500
for prior years		$19,500
Deduct: Dividends declared on 500 shares	$ 500	
common stock		
Dividends declared on 1,000 shares	1,000	1,500
preferred stock		
Retained Earnings, December 31, 198X		$18,000

REVENUE

Amount of money earned (which is collected [cash] and/or will be collected [accounts receivable]), from selling goods or services rendered (performed) for a specific period of time.

Under an accrual system a sale is recorded and recognized when the business earns it (whether money is collected or not).

(See matching concept)

Earned revenue results in an inward flow of assets (cash and/or accounts receivable).

REVENUE EXPENDITURE

After a business buys a plant asset (truck) certain expenditures (costs) will result in order to keep the plant asset at its "full usefulness" as determined by the business.

If the expenditures (costs) *only* help to keep the plant asset at its full usefulness for the *current accounting period* this is called a *revenue expenditure.*

(This expenditure is deducted from revenue on the year-end income statement as an expense.)

(See capital expenditure)

REVERSING ENTRY

A journal entry which *does not allow* certain expenses to be overstated (or too high) in a new accounting period.

This journal entry is just the *opposite or reversing* of an adjusting entry (which does not allow *certain* expenses to be understated [or too low] in the old accounting period).

Goal: Not to let a company's expenses in the new year appear to be higher than they really are.

Go to step "A," page 10 !!!

Reversing Entry

Steps

A. Go to page 10 and read about Jim Jackson.
B. Come back to this page to see how easy reversing entries really are.

   Do not go on until you have completed step A!!! Sorry for the inconvenience.

   Welcome back!

   Now let's see how:

   Jim will not *overstate* his expenses in the new year.

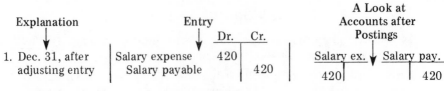

Explanation	Entry			A Look at Accounts after Postings
		Dr.	Cr.	
1. Dec. 31, after adjusting entry	Salary expense Salary payable	420	420	Salary ex. Salary pay. 420 420

The adjustment shows true expenses ($420) in old year.

2. Jan. 1, after closing entries	All temporary (expenses) accounts are cleaned up.	Salary ex. Salary pay. closed 420

The closing entries have cleaned up the temporary accounts (revenue, expenses, drawing, income summary).

3. Jan. 1, after reversing entry		Dr.	Cr.	Salary ex. Salary pay
	Salary payable Salary expense	420	420	420 420 | 420

Reversing entry will set up in step #4 expenses from being too high in the new year.

4. Jan. 8, paid regular payroll		Dr.	Cr.	Salary expense
	Salary expense Cash	700	700	700 | 420 (280) |

True expense of new year ($280). It is the reversing entry that puts a credit into the salaries expense ($420) to reduce or give a true picture of the actual expense in the new year when the regular payroll is paid (January 8).

If $420 was omitted, (salary expense) it would appear all $700
                        700
of salaries is an expense in the new year. We know that a part of the $700 is an expense of the old year. (As shown by the year-end adjusting entry.)

Insight: The reversing entries allow the bookkeeper to procede with the routine recording functions without having to recognize portions that were accrued.

RULES OF DEBITS AND CREDITS

		Increase	Decrease	Normal Balance
Assets	= Debit for increase, credit for decrease	debit	credit	debit
Liabilities	= Debit for decrease, credit for increase.	credit	debit	credit
Capital	= Debit for decrease, credit for increase	credit	debit	credit
Revenue	= Debit for decrease, credit for increase	credit	debit	credit
Expense	= Debit for increase, credit for decrease	debit	credit	debit
Drawing (withdrawal)	= Debit for increase, credit for decrease	debit	credit	debit

"or" between the two tables.

(Both say same thing)

Analyzing Business Transactions

1. What accounts are affected?

2. Are they going up or down?

3. Are they assets, liabilities, etc.?

4. Is it a debit or credit?

Assets	+	Expenses	+	Withdrawal	=	Liabilities	+	Capital	+	Revenue
Dr.	Cr.	Dr.	Cr.	Dr.	Cr.	Dr.	Cr.	Dr.	Cr.	Dr.	Cr.
+	−	+	−	+	−	−	+	−	+	−	+

SALARIES PAYABLE

We owe employees money for work they have done for us and have not been paid for yet. Salaries payable is a liability on the balance sheet.

(See accrued expenses)

Salaries Payable

Jim Brewer owns a minor league baseball team.

Business has been slow of late and Jim has not been able to pay wages to his ballplayers for the last month. Jim has created salaries payable.

SALES DISCOUNT

A savings off the regular price of a goods or services due to early payment of a bill by one's customers.

The sales discount (a debit balance) reduces the revenue (credit balance) a company collects and therefore reduces the total dollar amount of a company's sales. Sales discount is a company account found on the income statement.

(See sales returns and allowances)

Sales Discount

Jan. 5 Jim's Wholesale Lobster Co. sold on account $300 worth of lobsters to Moe Glass, Inc. Terms of sale were 2/10, N/30. (If Moe Glass pays within 20 days we [Jim's Wholesale] will give them a 2% reduction or $6 off the regular price.)

At the time of the sale Jim's Wholesale made the following entry:

Journal   Page #1

Date		Description (Accounts)	Folio (PR)	Debit	Credit
198X Jan.	5	Accounts rec.-Moe Glass	2	300	
		Sales	5		300

Jan. 8: Jim's Wholesale receives payment from Moe Glass and makes the following entry:

Journal   Page #2

Date		Description (Accounts)	Folio (PR)	Debit	Credit
198X Jan.	8	Cash	1	294	
		Sales discount	6	6	
		Acc. rec.-Moe Glass	2		300

(See purchase discount for comparison)

182

SALES JOURNAL

A book or place (special journal) where transactions are recorded *only* when sales are made *on account* (haven't received cash yet).

19XX   **Sales Journal**

Sept. 1 Invoice 109 to Miller & Co., $100

2 Sold merchandise on account to Mitchell and Mark Inc. invoice 633, for $2,000.

Date		Invoice Number	Accounts Debited	Folio (PR)	Accounts Rec. Debit Sales Credit
19XX Sept.	1	109	Miller and Co.	√	100
	2	633	Mitchell and Mark	√	2,000
			Totals		2,100

(10)   (20)

POSTING RULES

1. During the month (daily) post to each individual account (Miller & Co., Mitchell & Mark) in the accounts receivable subsidiary ledger. A check (√) is placed in the post reference column.

2. At the *end of the month* the total of $2,100 is posted to the general ledger as a *debit to accounts receivable* and credit to sales.

A/R   Sales
(Account Number 10)   (Account Number 20)

SALES RETURNS AND ALLOWANCES ACCOUNT

An account which shows the amount of merchandise or goods that a company or person (who isn't satisfied) returns or gets a partial allowance on price.

Sales have credit balances. Sales returns and allowances have debit balances or reduce the total sales of the company. Sales returns and allowances is a temporary account found on the income statement.

(See sales discounts)

Sales Returns and Allowances Account

On January 5, Jim's Wholesale Lobster Co., sold on account $300 worth of lobsters to Moe Glass Inc.

On January 6, Moe Glass issued a debit memo (reducing what they owed Jim's Wholesale) and returned $100 worth of lobsters to Jim's Wholesale because these lobsters were diseased.

Jim's Wholesale made the following entry (credit memo):

Journal   Page #1

Date		Description (accounts)	Folio (PR)	Debit	Credit
198X Jan.	1	Sales returns and allowances	10	100	
		Accounts receivable—M. Glass	5		100

(See debit or credit memo for back-up)

SALVAGE VALUE

A portion of the cost of a plant asset (equipment) that one can get back (from estimating market value) when it is removed or has reached the end of its productive life.

Salvage value is hard to estimate but can give us an estimate of how much depreciation should be taken on a plant asset (equipment) over its lifetime.

Equipment — salvage value = amount of depreciation to be taken over the life of a plant asset.

Salvage Value

Warren Ford bought a new truck for his sales fleet for $5,000.

Based on guidelines set up by the Internal Revenue, as well as past history of his other vehicles, Warren estimated in five years he could sell or trade the truck in the market place for $200.

Warren calculated he would depreciate the truck $4,800 over the next five years.

Truck	—	salvage value	=	amount to be depreciated
$5,000	—	$200	=	$4,800

184

SCHEDULE OF ACCOUNTS PAYABLE

A list of *individual* people or companies we owe money to (creditors).

The total of this list should equal the one figure in accounts payable (controlling account) in the general ledger after postings.

(See schedule of accounts receivable)

Schedule of Accounts Payable

Accounts Payable Ledger
(Subsidiary)

Cough Brothers

Date		Item	Folio (PR)	Debit	Credit	Balance Debit	Credit
Dec.	1		PJ 1		200		200
	10		CD 1	200		--------	--------

Ralph Brothers

Date		Item	Folio (PR)	Debit	Credit	Balance Debit	Credit
April	1		PJ 1		500		500

Smith Brothers

Date		Item	Folio (PR)	Debit	Credit	Balance Debit	Credit
May	10		PJ 1		300		300

Cashman Company
Schedule of Accounts Payable
December 31, 198X

Ralph Brothers	$500
Smith Brothers	300
Total accounts payable	$800*

*This will be balance in the accounts payable controlling account in the general ledger at the end of month.

SCHEDULE OF ACCOUNTS RECEIVABLE

A list of *individual* customers who owe us money. The total of the list should equal the one figure in accounts receivable (controlling accounts) in the general ledger after postings.

(See schedule of accounts payable)

Schedule of Accounts Receivable
Accounts Receivable Ledger
(Subsidiary)

Bush and Bee Inc.

Date		Item	Folio (PR)	Debit	Credit	Balance Debit	Credit
May	1		SJ 1	300		300	
			CR 1		300	---------	---------

Miller and Co.

Date		Item	Folio (PR)	Debit	Credit	Balance Debit	Credit
March	1		SJ 1	300		300	

Mitchell and Mark

Date		Item	Folio (PR)	Debit	Credit	Balance Debit	Credit
April	1		SJ 1	3,000		3,000	
			GJ 1		1,000	2,000	

Cashman Company
Schedule of Accounts Receivable
December 31, 198X

Miller and Co.	$ 300
Mitchell and Mark, Inc.	2,000
Total accounts receivable	$2,300*

*This will be the balance in the accounts receivable controlling account in the general ledger at end of month.

186

SCRAP VALUE

A portion of the cost of a plant asset (equipment) that one can get back when it is reached the end of its productive life.

Scrap value is hard to estimate but it gives us an estimate of how much depreciation should be taken on a plant asset (equipment) over its lifetime.

Equipment — scrap value = amount of depreciation to be taken over the lifetime of the plant asset

Scrap Value

Warren Ford bought a new truck for his sales fleet for $5,000.

Based on guidelines set up by the Internal Revenue, as well as past history of his other vehicles, Warren estimated in five years he could sell or trade the truck in the market place for $200.

Warren calculated he would depreciate the truck $4,800 over the next five years.

Truck — scrap value = amount to be depreciated
$5,000 $200 $4,800

SECURED BONDS

Bonds which are sold by a company that are backed up or secured by specifics asset(s) (buildings, equipment, etc.) of the company or other companies.

This becomes important if the company fails to pay off the bond when it comes due.

If this happens, the investor can go after what was secured on the bond.

Secured Bonds

Ron Hurley, holder of a secured bond, was quite concerned when the company failed to honor its obligation.

Ron went to his lawyer, who told him that the bond stated that in cases of nonpayment, the bond holder *is entitled* (Ron) to certain assets (equipment) of the company.

Ron felt much better.

SERIAL BONDS

All the bonds of a certain issue of a company *do not* come due (or mature) at once.

Parts of the bond issue mature or come due for payment at *different* times.

Serial Bonds

James Stores, Inc., who had raised money for plant expansion by selling serial bonds (January 196X), issued the following dates when portions of its $100,000 bond issue will be paid back:

		Serial Numbers
January 197X	$ 25,000	1-250
January 198X	25,000	251-500
January 199X	25,000	501-750
January 200X	25,000	751-1000
	$100,000	

By January 200X, all bonds will be paid back (here interest has not been discussed).

SINKING FUND BONDS

Bonds that require that a special reserve or fund be set up (to accumulate money) that will make sure the company *will be able* to pay off the bonds *when they become due* (reach maturity).

Sinking Fund Bonds

Jangles, Inc., in need of paying off current debts, issued $100,000 worth of sinking fund bonds at 6% for 10 years to investors.

The stipulation with the bonds was that each year Jangles, Inc. must set up a sinking fund which accumulates the money (appr. $10,000 per year) in order to make sure the company will be able to meet its obligations when the bonds come due.

Jangles, Inc. could invest money from the sinking fund in *relatively stable* income (money) producing securities.

188

SIX PERCENT, 60-DAY METHOD

A shortcut method of calculating interest (or the cost of using someone else's money) instead of the traditional formula of:

P	X	R	X	T	=	Interest
(Principal)		(Rate of Interest)		(Time)		(Interest)

The 6% 60-day method will only be a shortcut if the math doesn't get too complicated.

Six Percent, 60-Day Method

What is the interest on $1,200 at 6% for 20 days?

6% 60 Day Method	Traditional Method
1. 6% (per year) for 60 days (1/6 of a year) is equal to 1%	$I = \$1,200 \times .06 \times \dfrac{20}{360}$
2. 6% for 60 days on $1,200 = $12.00 (1% x $1,200 = $12.00)	$I = \$1,200 \times .06 \times \dfrac{1}{18}$
3. 6% for 20 days on $1,200 = $\dfrac{1}{3}(12)$ or $4.00	$I = 72 \times \dfrac{1}{18} = \$4.00$
4. Review: A. 6% 60 days $1,200 = $12.00 B. 6% 20 days $1,200 = $\dfrac{1}{3}$ of "A" = $4.00	$I = \$4.00$

SLIDE

An error in writing a number by adding or deleting zeroes.

Slide

$542 = $54.20
Five hundred and forty-two was written as fifty-four dollars and twenty cents by mistake.

SOLE PROPRIETORSHIP*

A business owned by one person.

SPECIAL JOURNALS

A book or place (journal) where groups of similar transactions (like those involving paying of cash) are recorded.

By using *special journals*, speed and accuracy, as well as organization, may result rather than putting all transactions into one *general journal*.

Special Journals

Sales journal————————— Sale of merchandise on account

Cash receipt journal———————— Receiving money from any source

Purchase journal————————— Buying anything on account

Cash payments (disburse-————— Money being paid for any purments) journal pose

Check register————————— Paying bills using a voucher system.

Payroll register————————— Records payroll
(if not used as a
supplementary record)

*Other forms would be partnerships and corporations.

190

STATED VALUE OF STOCK

An estimated figure of value which is assigned to a corporation's stock by its board of directors. Sometimes the board of directors designates an assigned stated value to stock with no pay value.

Not all states require a par value to be placed on a corporation's stock.

(See par value for further discussion)

Stated Value of Stock

On January 8, 197X, Howard Caras Sweaters Inc. issued 5,000 shares of no-par common stock at a stated value of $5 for $15 per share.

The following entry was recorded:

Journal   Page #1

Date	Description (Accounts)	Folio (PR)	Debit	Credit
198X Jan. 8	Cash		75,000	
	Common stock			25,000
	Paid-in capital in excess of stated value			50,000

5,000 shares X $15 per share

5,000 shares X $ 5 per share

STATEMENT ANALYSIS

Taking financial reports (or statements) and trying to hopefully interpret or better understand the operations and financial position of a company as of a specific period of time or as of a certain date.

(See comparative, vertical, or horizontal for more detail)

STOCK
Basic Ownership in a Corporation

A. *To an Investor*

This is a piece of paper(s) (called stock certificates) which show the amount or ownership and rights one has in a corporation.

Depending upon the type of stock as well as the amount purchased, different amounts of rights and ownership will develop.

B. *To a Corporation*

This is a means or way of raising money (capital) by selling shares of stock to investors.

Stock

Mighty Wool Inc., issued 1,000 shares of $10 par stock to investors at $20 per share.

A. *To an Investor*

One now has bought ownership and rights into Mighty Wool (depending on amount bought).

B. *To the Corporation*

Mighty Wool Inc., has raised $20,000 (1,000 shares X $20 per share) by selling some stock.

STOCK CERTIFICATE

Piece(s) of paper(s) which shows or verifies the amount of ownership and rights one (stockholder) has in a corporation.

(See preferred stock)

Courtesy of E.F. Hutton.

STOCK DIVIDEND

The amount of stock that a corporation divides or gives out to the stockholders of the corporation without receiving money from the stock given out.

There is *no* cash being given to the stockholders.

The corporation transfers or takes an amount from retained earnings (accumulated earnings) and places it into paid-in capital.

This means earnings are kept in the corporation instead of being paid out as in a cash dividend.

(See stock split)

Stock Dividend

Joanne Soterpolus owns 1,000 shares of Beep Corporation.

On July 10, she received notice of a 5% stock dividend issued by the company.

Joanne was thrilled, but her best friend Kath Spaneas, told her "Don't be too excited, the company is giving all the stockholders a 5% dividend, which means you really own the same proportion of the corporation as before."

Before	*After*
1,000 shares $= \dfrac{1}{100}$ of all stock	1,050 $= \dfrac{1}{100}$ of all stock

STOCK SPLIT

A method usually used by a corporation to reduce the market price of their common stock that would hopefully cause more people to invest in it. The stock split is the issuance of a large number of shares to stockholders when no new assets are contributed to firm.

The method reduces the par value of the corporation's common stock.

The corporation can then issue more common stock to the stockholders to make up for the reduction in par value.

(See stock dividend)

Stock Split

The stock of Baby Industries (50,000 shares issued at $20 par) was selling on the stock exchange for $200 per share.

The board of directors of Baby Industries declared a two-for-one stock split (with the idea of reducing the price of the stock to $100) to encourage more investors to buy the stock.

Corporation Stock Structure

Before Split	*After Split*
50,000 shares at $20 par	100,000 shares at $10 par

Before

John Mills originally owned *100 shares* of Baby Industries at a market value of *$200 per share*, or his total value of his stock was $200,000.

After

John now has *200 shares* at a market value of *$100 per share*, or his stock is worth $200,000.

Things haven't changed

195

STOCKHOLDERS (SHAREHOLDERS)

The owners of a corporation.

The owners have bought or have received shares of stock that show the amount of their ownership and rights in a company.

One must keep in mind that a corporation, in the eyes of the law, is separate from its owner.

The corporation is an artificial person in the eyes of the law.

Keep in mind individuals and companies can be stockholders.

STOCKHOLDER'S EQUITY (CAPITAL)
(SHAREHOLDER'S EQUITY)

Claims of the owners of a corporation (who have bought or received stock) to things or assets in that corporation.

These rights of the owners vary depending on what type of stock the owner has (common stock, preferred stock, etc.).

Stockholder's Equity	=	Paid-in Capital	+	Retained Earnings
(For the usuals, see paid-in cap. for help)		Usually the amount of money that a corp. rec. from selling (or issuing) stock to investors		The profit that has been kept or has accumulated in the business rather than being paid out (dividends, etc.)

Stockholder's Equity (Shareholder's Equity)

Paid-in capital (contributed capital):

Common stock.	$200,000	
Retained earnings	40,000	
Total stockholders' equity		$240,000

196

STRAIGHT-LINE METHOD OF DEPRECIATION

A method used to spread (or allocate) the total amount of depreciation related to a plant asset (equipment, building, etc.) over its estimated life.

This method spreads the depreciation expense equally over a number of years (the life estimation of the asset).

$$\frac{\text{Cost of plant asset} - \text{salvage value}}{\text{Number of years to be depreciated}} = \frac{\text{depreciation expense}}{\text{taken each year}}$$

(See declining-balance, sum-of-years, and units of production)

Straight-Line Method of Depreciation

Facts:

1. Tremblay Corporation bought a truck for $5,000.
2. Residual (scrap, trade-in, etc.) value is $500.
3. Estimated life, 9 years.

$$\text{Annual depreciation} = \frac{\$5,000 - \$500}{9 \text{ years}} = \$500 \text{ per/year}$$

	Depreciation	Accumulated Depreciation at End of Each Year	Book Value
Year 1	$500	$ 500	$4,500
2	500	1,000	4,000
3	500	1,500	3,500
4	500	2,000	3,000
5	500	2,500	2,500
6	500	3,000	2,000
7	500	3,500	1,500
8	500	4,000	1,000
9	500	4,500	500

SUBSCRIPTIONS (RECEIVABLE)

One way or method a corporation uses to sell its stock (especially when a corporation has just been organized).

1. Under this method, the investor subscribes or "signs up" for a certain amount of stock.

   The investor promises to pay the corporation for the stock in the future (one payment or installment).

   The corporation then has an asset called *common stock subscriptions receivable.*

2. *After* the corporation receives full payment from the investor, the corporation issues the stock certificate(s).

Subscriptions (Receivable)

John Dunn Corporation received subscriptions for 5,000 shares of $5 par common stock from investors (subscribers) at $6 per share, with a down payment of 50% of the subscription price.

					Explanation
March	1	Com. Stock Sub. Rec.	30,000		5,000 Shrs. @ $6/Shr. = $30,000
		Common Stock Sub.		25,000	5,000 Shrs. @ $5/Shr. = $25,000
		Premium on Com. Stk.		5,000	30,000 − 25,000 = 5,000 Pre.
(Down	1	Cash	15,000		2,500 Shrs. × $6/Per Shr.
Payment)		Common Stk. Sub. Rec.		15,000	= $15,000

Received 25% of subscription price from all subscribers.

May	1	Cash	7,500		1,250 Shrs. × $6/Per Share
		Common Stk. Sub. Rec.		7,500	= $7,500

Received final 25% of subscription price from all subscribers and issued the stock certificates.

July	1	Cash	7,500		1,250 Shrs. × $6/Per Share
		Common Stk. Sub. Rec.		7,500	= $7,500
	1	Common Stock Subscribed	25,000		5,000 Shrs. × $5/Per Share
		Common Stock		25,000	= $25,000

SUBSIDIARY COMPANY

A business owned and controlled by another company (called the parent company).

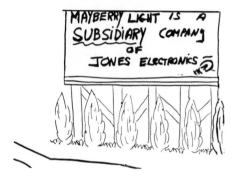

Jones Electric owns 80% of the stock of Mayberry Light.

SUM-OF-THE-YEARS-DIGIT METHOD OF DEPRECIATION

A method used to spread (or allocate) the total amount of depreciation related to a plant asset (equipment, building, etc.) over its estimated life.

This method is similar to the declining-balance method in that it *takes more or accelerates depreciation in the early years of the plant asset,* but this method does its calculations on a fractional basis (sum of number of years to be depreciated = denominator and years left to be depreciated is the numerator) versus the declining-balance which uses a percentage rate.

This method *uses* salvage value. (residual value).

(See declining-balance method)

Sum-of-the-Years-Digit Method of Depreciation

Facts: Cost of truck $31,000
Residual value 1,000
Estimated life 5 years

Year	Cost, Less Residual X Rate*	Depreciation Expense for Year	Accumulated Depreciation End of Year	Book Value End of Year (Cost-accu. dep.)
1	30,000 X 5/15	$10,000	$10,000	$21,000 (31,000 − 10,000)
2	30,000 X 4/15	8,000	$18,000 (10,000 + 8,000)	$13,000 (31,000 − 18,000)
3	30,000 X 3/15	6,000	$24,000 (18,000 + 6,000)	$ 7,000 (31,000 − 24,000)
4	30,000 X 2/15	4,000	$28,000 (24,000 + 4,000)	$ 3,000 (31,000 − 28,000)
5	30,000 X 1/15	2,000	$30,000 (28,000 + 2,000)	$ 1,000 (31,000 − 30,000)

$$*5 + 4 + 3 + 2 + 1 = 15 \text{ or } s = \frac{N(N+1)}{2} = \frac{5(5+1)}{2} = \frac{5(6)}{2} = 15$$

SUNDRY ACCOUNT COLUMN (MISCELLANEOUS ACCOUNT)

A column in a journal which records parts of miscellaneous transactions (or transactions that do not occur too often).*

Cash Receipts Journal			Page 1
Accounts Credited	PR	Sundry Cr.	
R. Jones Capital	310	120,000	

Notes Payable	212	110,000	
Totals		130,000	
		(X)	

*If transactions occurs too often a special column would be set up not to abuse the sundry column.

T-ACCOUNT

A simplified device or place for demonstration that looks like the letter "T" which records and summarizes individual accounts (asset, liability, capital [owner's equity], revenue, expenses, drawing); also income summary (expenses and revenue summary).

(See account)

T-Account

Cash			Account No. 1	
Jan. 1	Bal.	10	Nov. 1	5
Jan. 10		15		

TERM BONDS

All bonds of a certain issue come due (or mature) at once.

Term Bonds

Jon Lynch Inc. had raised money for plant expansion, as well as paying off current debts by selling term bonds ($100,000 worth, at 6% per year payable on January 1, 198X).

On January 1, 198X, Jon Lynch Inc. paid back the $100,000. (Or we say the bonds issued had come due *all at once*).

TRADE DISCOUNTS

Reductions from the list or retail price offered by many manufacturers and wholesalers.

A trade discount has *no relation* to cash discount, which deals with prompt payment.

Trade Account

Gem Wholesalers offered rings for $2,000 (with a trade discount of 10%) to its customers.

$2,000   X   10%   = $200 Trade Discount
$2,000   — $200   = $1,800

Selling price of ring before discount

$2,000

Trade Discount

$200

Selling price of ring after discount

$1,800

Key Point: Trade discounts are not recorded.

TRADE-IN VALUE

A portion of the cost of a plant asset (equipment) that one can get back when it is removed or has reached the end of its productive life.

Trade-in value is hard to estimate but gives us an estimate of how much depreciation should be taken on a plant asset (equipment) over its lifetime.

Equipment — trade-in value = amount of depreciation to be taken over the lifetime of the plant asset.

Trade-In Value

Warren Ford bought a new truck for his sales fleet for $5,000.

Based on guidelines set up by the Internal Revenue, as well as past history of his other vehicles, Warren estimated in five years he could sell or trade the truck in the market place for $200.

Warren calculated he would depreciate the truck $4,800 over the next 5 years.

Truck — trade-in value = amount to be depreciated
$5,000 $200 $4,800

TRANSACTIONS

Happenings in a business which change its financial position or makeup. You take the transaction and record it in a journal. (A book or place where transactions are first recorded.)

Transactions

Buy a house
Pay college tuition
Make a sale in a store
Buy equipment

Buy some supplies
Invest money in a business
Withdraw money out of a business

TRANSPOSITION

Rearranging digits by mistake.

Transposition

Writing five hundred and forty-two as four hundred and fifty-two by mistake.

$$542 = 452$$

TREASURY STOCK

The corporations *own* stock that has been *bought back* (by the corporation) or has been given back to the corporation as a gift.

This stock had previously been issued (or sold) to investors who had fully paid for it.

This stock hasn't been cancelled nor has it been reissued again.

Treasury stock is not an asset. It loses many of the rights of common stock.

Treasury Stock

On February 1, 197X, Maybelled Corporation bought back 2,000 shares of its stock from investors for $50 per share. The following was recorded:

Journal   Page #1

Date		Description (Accounts)	Folio (PR)	Debit	Credit
197X					
Feb.	1	Treasury stock	22	100,000	
		Cash	1		100,000

Treasury stock reduces stockholder's equity. It would be shown on the balance sheet as follows.

Stockholder's Equity

Paid-in capital	$100,000
Common stock 10 par,	
100,000 shares	
Retained earnings	50,000
Total	$150,000
Deduct treasury stock (2,000	− 100,000
shares @ $50 per share)	
Total stockholder's equity	$ 50,000

TRIAL BALANCE

A list of the ledger (group of accounts) to test equality of debits and credits.

(See post-closing trial balance)

Trial Balance

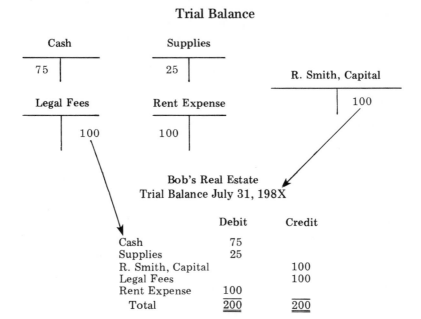

(The trial balance is listed in the following order: assets, liabilities, capital, withdrawals, revenue, and expenses.)

UNADJUSTED TRIAL BALANCE

The trial balance (list of the ledger) *before* it is updated by adjusting entries.

(See: adjusted trial balance, adjusting entries)

Unadjusted Trial Balance

December 31, 198X

	Debit	Credit
Cash	100	
Accounts receivable	200	
Supplies	300	
Equipment	400	
Accumulated depreciation—equipment		100
J. Smith, capital		100
J. Smith, withdrawal	200	
Legal fees		1,000
Total	1,200	1,200

Actually, supplies should be $200 ($100 of supplies had been used up during the year) and accumulated depreciation should be $200 ($100 of depreciation taken each year on equipment). These will be updated by adjusting entries which will then form the following adjusted trial balance.

Adjusted Trial Balance

	Debit	Credit
Cash	100	
Accounts receivable	200	
Supplies	200	
Equipment	400	
Accumulated depreciation—equipment		200
J. Smith, capital		100
J. Smith, withdrawal	200	
Legal fees		1,000
Supplies expense	100	
Depreciation expense	100	
Total	1,300	1,300

UNDERWRITER

Dealers or brokers in investment companies that buy stocks or bonds (type of securities) from a corporation with the intent to *resell* these securities to the public.

Underwriter

James Securities, an underwriter, bought a new issue of stock from Mick's Department Store.

This stock, James Securities will *resell* to investors at a higher price.

The result being Mick's Department Store didn't have to worry about selling their stock to many different investors, while James Securities makes a profit from reselling the stock to investors.

UNEARNED REVENUE

A *liability* which results when a company receives *money in advance* for a sale before the company delivers the goods or service. The company postpones recognizing the sale until they *earn it.*

Unearned Revenue

January 1: *Spice* magazine received $100 from Pam Sisto for payment of a one-year subscription to *Spice.*

Since *Spice* magazine hadn't really earned *any* of the sale (until they start sending the magazine), the following entry was recorded by *Spice*:

Journal   Page #1

Date	Description (Accounts)	Folio (PR)	Debit	Credit
198X Dec. 31	Cash	1	100	
	Unearned revenue	10		100

Unearned revenue is a liability—*Spice owes* a service to Pam Sisto (a *liability* called unearned revenue). Unearned revenue is a *liability* and not a sale.

When *Spice* earns the sale, or part of the sale, they will reduce their *liability* (by a debit to unearned revenue) and will show a sale (a credit to earned revenue).

Remember, unearned revenue is a liability.

Spice postpones the recognition of a sale until they *earn* it.

UNITS-OF-PRODUCTION (OUTPUT) METHOD OF DEPRECIATION

A method used to spread (or allocate) the total amount of depreciation related to a plant asset (equipment) over its *estimated production* life.

This method estimates the depreciation based on the units of production by a machine (plant asset). The formula used is:

$$\frac{\text{Cost of plant asset } - \text{ Salvage}}{\begin{array}{l}\text{Total estimate of the units of}\\ \text{production for the lifetime of}\\ \text{the plant asset}\\ \text{(Life hours of machine)}\end{array}} = \begin{array}{l}\text{Depreciation taken per}\\ \text{unit of production (or}\\ \text{hours machine has run)}\end{array}$$

Units-of-Production Method of Depreciation

Facts:
Machine cost = $10,000
Salvage = $ 1,000
Life hours of machine = 9,000 hours

$$\frac{\$10,000 - \$1,000}{9,000} = \$1.00 \text{ an hour}$$

If machine runs for 200 hours the first year $200 ($1.00/per hour X 200 hours) of depreciation will result.

UNLIMITED LIABILITY

If a business (not corporation) falls into debt the owner(s) of that business may be *liable* for paying or settling the debts of the business from his *own* personal assets (savings accounts, home, car).

(For comparison, see limited liability)

Unlimited Liability

Jim's Sporting Goods (a sole proprietorship) opened for business on January 1, 197X.

On June 1, 197X, Jim's Sporting Goods faced heavy losses and was forced to go out of business.

Jim had so many bills to pay (the creditors) that he was forced to sell *his home* in order to pay off the *debts* of the business.

VERTICAL ANALYSIS OF STATEMENTS

One way of understanding or interpreting comparative statements.

This way will hopefully give a better understanding of the operations and financial position of a company as of a specific period of time, or as of a certain date.

This method relates or groups each figure to a base figure (going down the columns).

(See example)

(See horizontal analysis, comparative statements)

Vertical Analysis of Statements

	1985		1984	
	Am't	Perc. *	Am't	Perc. **
Assets				
Current assets	25	25%	10	20%
Long-term investments	20	20%	20	40%
Plant assets	20	20%	10	20%
Intangible assets	35	35%	10	20%
Total assets	100	100%	50	100%
Liabilities				
Current liabilities	10	10%	5	10%
Long-term liabilities	20	20%	20	40%
Total liabilities	30	30%	25	50%
Stockholder's equity				
Common stock	50	50%	20	40%
Retained earnings	20	20%	5	10%
Total stockholder's equity	70	70%	25	50%
Total liabilities and stockholder's equity	100	100%	50	100%

$*\dfrac{25}{100} = 25\%$ (base figure)

$**\dfrac{10}{50} = 20\%$ (base figure)

$***\dfrac{5}{50} = 10\%$ (base figure)

VOUCHER

(See voucher register, check register)

Voucher

Voucher Art Calnan Auto Supplies, Inc.		
Date July 1, 1985		Voucher Number 430
Payee Rowe Company		
3 Essex Street		
Beverly, Ma. 01915		

Date	Details	Amount
July 1, 1985	Invoice No. 2333 FOB Beverly 2/10, n/30	$300.00
	Attach supporting documents	

VOUCHERS PAYABLE

Vouchers Payable (Accounts Payable)

John Mizex Corporation (which uses a voucher system) bought $500 of merchandise on account from Kendal Rens.

The following was entered into the voucher register:
(1) A debit to purchases
(2) A credit to vouchers payable (that we owe money)

Purchases	Vouchers Payable
500	500

VOUCHER REGISTER

When a company uses a voucher system the *voucher register* takes the place of the *purchase journal*.

Any expense or purchase that will require payment (cash or check) will be recorded into the voucher (an expanded type of purchase journal) register.

(See check register)

Voucher Register

Date	Voucher Number	Payee (One Who Will Receive Money)	Payment Date	Check #	Voucher Payable Credit	Purchs. (Debits)	Freight (Debits)	Miscellaneous Accounts Debit Ac. Name Am't
Feb.								
10	3	Katz Rlt.	3/10	911	$300	$300		
12	5	Russell	3/12	912	350	300	$50	
15	8	J.P. Stationery	3/15	913	200			Off. Sup. $200

1. We bought merchandise from Katz Realty for resale for $300 on Feb. 10. We paid off (or reduced voucher payable by $300) by writing a check from our check register on March 10.

2. We bought merchandise from Russell Sales for $300 (plus $50 for freight) on Feb. 12. We paid off (or reduced vouchers payable by $350) by writing a check from our check register on March 12.

3. We bought supplies (not for resale) from J.P. Stationery on Feb. 15. We paid off (or reduced vouchers payable by $200) by writing a check.

(See check register for comparison)

VOUCHER SYSTEM

A type of internal control system (usually for a large company) which controls the cash (checks) being spent (or written).

This system tells the person paying the bills (obligations) that these obligations are true and proper and should be paid.

(See internal control)

Voucher System

Made up of:

 Vouchers
 Voucher file (paid and unpaid)
 Voucher register (takes place of purchase journal)
 Check register (takes place of cash disbursements journal)
 General journal

(See individual item for detail)

W-2

A statement sent or given to an employee (worker) of a business which shows the gross earnings and deductions (FICA, Federal Income Tax) for a calendar year which is used for income tax purposes.

The business sends a copy of the W-2 to the state, as well as the Internal Revenue.

The worker attaches a copy of the W-2 to his Federal and State Income Tax Returns.

(See calendar year, W-4)

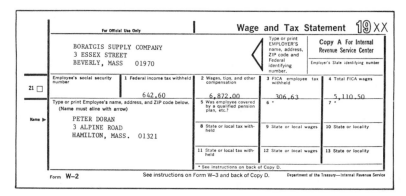

W-4

A form (filled out by a new employee, or an old employee who wants to change the figures in the form) which provides the proper information to the business to calculate a worker's (employee's) net pay (gross pay — deductions).

(See W-2)

Form **W-4** (Rev. May 1977) Department of the Treasury Internal Revenue Service	**Employee's Withholding Allowance Certificate** (Use for Wages Paid After May 31, 1977) This certificate is for income tax withholding purposes only. It will remain in effect until you change it. If you claim exemption from withholding, you will have to file a new certificate on or before April 30 of next year.		
Type or print your full name MURRAY KATZ		Your social security number 021 36 9494	
Home address (number and street or rural route) 26 SABLE ROAD	Marital Status	☐ Single ☐ Married ☐ Married, but withhold at higher Single rate	
City or town, State, and ZIP code SALEM, MASS. 01970		Note: If married, but legally separated, or spouse is a nonresident alien, check the single block.	

1 Total number of allowances you are claiming . . . . | 1

2 Additional amount, if any, you want deducted from each pay (if your employer agrees) . . . . | $

3 I claim exemption from withholding (see instructions). Enter "Exempt" . . . .

Under the penalties of perjury, I certify that the number of withholding exemptions and allowances claimed on this certificate does not exceed the number to which I am entitled. If claiming exemption from withholding, I certify that I incurred no liability for Federal income tax for last year and that I anticipate that I will incur no liability for Federal income tax for this year.

Signature ▶ *Murray Katz*   Date ▶ 12/21   , 19 7X

Key Point: The W-4 doesn't provide information for deductions for savings, bonds, hospitalization, union dues, etc.

214

WEIGHTED AVERAGE OF INVENTORY COSTING

A method used to assign a cost or place or dollar figure to the goods remaining (ending inventory) in a business at the end of a period of time and to find the *cost of the goods a business sold* during that same period of time.

This method gets a *weighted average cost per unit** of all inventory (beginning inventory plus all purchases).

(See LIFO, FIFO)

Weighted Average of Inventory Costing

J.J. Supermarket

Facts:	No. of Cans of Soup Bought for Resale	Cost Per Can	Total Cost
On Jan. 1, 198X	20	$3.00	$ 60.00
March 1	15	2.00	30.00
Nov. 3	10	1.00	10.00
Nov. 10	55	2.00	110.00
	100		$210.00

Weighted average cost per unit = total no. of $\dfrac{\text{total cost}}{\text{cans of soup}}$ bought

$$= \frac{210}{100}$$

$$= \$2.10 \text{ is to average cost of bring-}$$
ing all the soup into the store (per can of soup)

If at the end of the year 5 cans of soup are left in the store the cost of these cans are calculated as follows:

$2.10 X 5 cans = $10.50 cost of ending inventory.

*(See example on how to calculate weighted average cost per unit.)

WITHDRAWAL (DRAWINGS)

The money or assets an owner takes out of his business for his own *personal* satisfaction (living expense). *It is not a business expense* (such as salaries) but a *personal* expense. Withdrawals have a debit balance and are *not* found on the income statement.

In a corporation withdrawals are *sometimes* called dividends.

Withdrawal (Drawings)

John Fling withdrew $100 from the business for a personal family trip.

WORK IN PROCESS ACCOUNT—MANUFACTURING COMPANY (GOODS IN PROCESS)

One type* of inventory account in a manufacturing business that contains information about goods that are now in the process of being manufactured, or what is the work in process.

(See also direct labor or factory overhead)

*The other two types of inventory: 1. Raw materials.
                                                    2. Finished goods.

216

WORKING CAPITAL

Current assets minus current liabilities.

(See fund statement)

Working Capital

Current assets:	
Cash	$1,000
Accounts receivable	500
Inventory	300
Prepaid rent	500
Total current assets	$2,300
Current liabilities:	
Accounts payable	$ 400
Notes payable	800
Total current liabilities	$1,200

```
  Total current assets
– Total current liabilities
= Working capital
```

WORK SHEET

An accounting form or paper which acts as a tool in gathering and summarizing, in an orderly process, accounting data on a sheet of paper that is needed in completing the accounting cycle (preparing a trial balance, adjusting entries, clearing or closing entries, preparing financial statements—balance sheet and income statement).

Work sheet can be compared to a *rough draft that one uses in writing a term paper.* When the completed project (like a balance sheet) is turned in, no one sees the "scrap paper" (which made the final outcome possible—like a work sheet).

Jeff Slater
Worksheet
December 31, 19XX

Account Titles	Trial Balance Debit	Trial Balance Credit	Adjustments Debit	Adjustments Credit	Adj. Trial Balance Debit	Adj. Trial Balance Credit	Income Statement Debit	Income Statement Credit	Balance Sheet Debit	Balance Sheet Credit
Cash	3000 00				3000 00				3000 00	
Accounts receivable	1500 00				1500 00				1500 00	
Merchandise inventory*	7000 00				7000 00		7000 00	1000 00	1000 00	
Prepaid rent	500 00			(a) 150 00	350 00				350 00	
Office supplies	600 00			(b) 230 00	370 00				370 00	
Store supplies	350 00				350 00				350 00	
Prepaid advertising	150 00			(c) 33 00	117 00				117 00	
Office furniture	10000 00				10000 00				10000 00	
Office equipment	4800 00				4800 00				4800 00	
Accumulated depreciation—off. equ.		200 00		(d) 600 00		800 00				800 00
Salaries payable		240 00		(e) 1000 00		1240 00				1240 00
Accounts payable		6650 00	(f) 700 00			5950 00				5950 00
Jeff Slater, capital		10000 00				10000 00				10000 00
Sales		27710 00				27710 00		27710 00		
Sales returns and allowances	700 00				700 00		700 00			
Sales discounts	150 00				150 00		150 00			
Purchases	12000 00				12000 00		12000 00			
Purchases discount		600 00				600 00		600 00		
Freight-in	450 00				450 00		450 00			
Salaries expense	4200 00		(e) 1000 00		5200 00		5200 00			
Rent expense			(a) 150 00		150 00		150 00			
Office supplies expense			(b) 230 00		230 00		230 00			
Advertising expense			(c) 33 00		33 00		33 00			
Depreciation expense—off. equip.			(d) 600 00		600 00		600 00			
Purchases returns and allowances				(f) 700 00		700 00		700 00		
	45400 00	45400 00	2713 00	2713 00	47000 00	47000 00	26513 00	30010 00	21487 00	17990 00
Net income (net profit)							3497 00			3497 00
							30010 00	30010 00	21487 00	21487 00

*The $7,000 of beginning merchandise inventory is assumed to be a cost and thus is placed on the debit column of the income statement on the worksheet and the ending figure for merchandise inventory ($1,000) is assumed not to be sold and thus not a cost. This ending inventory figure is the beginning inventory on the debit column of the balance sheet.

Crossword Puzzles and Accounting Hunt*

*Solutions can be found at end of this section.

1. Rule of Debits and Credits, Categories and Normal Balances

Across:

2. An increase in an asset called cash is done by a _____.
3. _____ depreciation is a contra asset with a credit balance.
7. Accounts receivable is an _____.
8. Sales (revenue) normally has a _____ balance.
9. _____, which shows rights of the owner has a normal balance of a credit.
14. A debit to salaries indicates an _____.
16. A debit to prepaid rent indicates an _____.
17. Accounts payable is a _____.
19. A credit to accumulated depreciation is an _____ to that contra-account.
21. Supplies consumed in the operations of a business becomes an _____ which is increased by a debit.
22. _____ rent is an asset with a normal debit balance.
24. A _____ to drawings increases the account.
26. Accumulated depreciation is a contra-_____.
29. Abbreviation for debit is _____.
30. An _____ in notes payable is a credit.
31. Cash has a _____ balance and is an asset.
32. _____ is a current asset.
33. The contra _____ of an equipment account for depreciation is accumulated depreciation.
34. The T-_____ is used for demonstration purposes.

Down:

1. A debit to salaries payable means we have _____ the amount owed.
2. An increase in withdrawals is a _____.
4. The _____ normal balance of cash is a debit.
5. Accounts payable is a _____.
6. The _____ balance on an expense is a debit.
10. _____ earnings has credit balance (usually).
11. Revenue is decreased by a _____.
12. A _____ in a liability is by a debit.
13. A _____ to retained earnings reduces the account.
15. A _____ to accounts receivable is an increase.
18. A _____ to equipment increases the account.
20. _____ have a normal balance of a debit and are costs incurred in making sales.

23. Unearned rent is a liability which is reduced by a _____.
25. Withdrawal is a nonbusiness _____ with a normal balance of a debit.
26. Prepaid insurance is an _____ with a normal balance of a debit.
27. Accumulated depreciation is an _____ account.
28. Retained earnings has a normal balance of a _____.
29. A _____ to drawings does not increase the "business" expenses. Drawings are a nonbusiness expense.

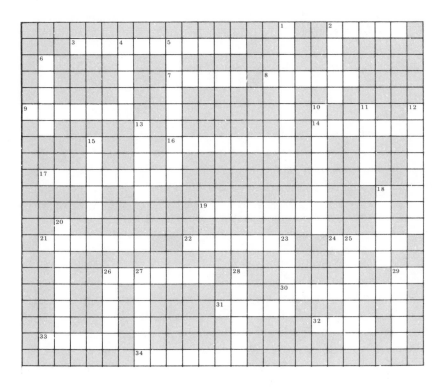

2. Adjusting and Closing Entries

Across:

1. _____ are usually closed directly to capital (owner equity).
6. Unearned revenue is a _____ (use abbreviation).
7. When _____ is taken, it is an expense and it also increases accumulated depreciation.
9. Adjustments bring certain _____ accounts up or down to their correct or true balance.
10. Rent paid in advance is classified as a _____ _____.
12. Adjustments effect _____ _____.
14. Supplies used up is a _____ to a business.
16. The _____ balance of drawings is a debit.
17. _____ is transferred to E & R (income summary).
19. When E & R (income summary) has a _____ _____ it will decrease capital.
22. When expenses are greater than revenue, a _____ results.
24. _____ -expenses = net income.
25. The abbreviation for liability is _____.
26. _____ revenue is not a sale, but a liability.
27. _____ _____ _____ entries take all the temporary accounts and summarize their effects on capital or retained earnings.

Down:

2. Earned management fees is _____.
3. Prepaid insurance is an _____.
4. Closing entries summarize the effects of temporary accounts on _____.
5. _____ have a normal balance of a debit.
7. When retained earnings has a debit balance a _____ results.
8. An _____ _____ results when an expense accumulates or builds up that is not recorded or paid for, but really represents an expense in the old year.
11. _____ usually are closed out by credits to the individual ledger accounts.
13. Revenue or _____ is closed to income summary (E + R summary).
15. A nonbusiness expense is called a _____.
18. Capital has a _____ balance of credit.
20. Revenue earned minus the _____ incurred in earning the revenue = net income under the accrual system.
21. Income _____ has a normal balance of credit when their is a profit.
23. Income _____ is used to transfer expenses and revenues to capital.

3. Journals

Across:

1. The _____ journal is a place where groups of similar transactions are recorded.

5. In a journal the _____ column shows the number of the account to which information has been or will be transferred (posted) to a ledger.

8. The _____ _____ journal shows the outflow or spending of cash (check) in recording business transactions.

9. The subsidiary_____is not found in the general ledger.

10. The _____ journal records sales made on account.

11. The _____ payable ledger (subsidiary) contains the records of individual people or companies we owe money to.

13. _____ _____ show the amount of merchandise or goods that a company or person (who is not satisfied) returns.

14. The transferring of information from a journal to a ledger is called _____ .

15. The _____ _____ account shows the amount of merchandise returned to suppliers for defective or returned goods.

17. An other name for the cash payments journal is cash _____ .

18. The accounts receivable controlling account should equal the sum of the accounts receivable_____ ledger.

Down:

2. The _____ journal is a place where transactions are recorded when buying something on account.

3. An error in writing a number by adding or deleting zeroes is called a _____.

4. Books or places where transactions are first put or recorded are called _____ .

6. The _____ _____ journal records transactions when money (check) is received from any source.

7. The accounts payable controlling account is found in the _____ ledger.

12. The _____ of accounts receivable is a *list* of individual customers who owe us money.

16. The _____ column of a journal records parts of miscellaneous transactions, (transactions that do not occur too often).

4. Accruals and Deferrals

Across:

2. _____ _____ of accounting is the opposite of accrual basis of accounting.

4. Unearned revenue is a _____ .

6. Earned _____ -expenses incurred in earning that revenue = net income.

7. A deferral postpones the recognition of a sale (although you have already _____ the money) until you earn it.

8. Earned revenue — incurred expenses = _____ _____ .

12. A _____ to unearned revenue reduces the liability.

13. An accrued _____ is an expense that is accumulating or building up that is not recorded or paid for but really represents an expense in the old year.

14. An expense does not have to be_____ in cash to be recognized as an expense in an accrual system.

16. Earned revenue- _____ expenses try to fulfill the matching principle in an attempt to arrive at a true picture of net income.

17. An adjusting _____ is needed many times to bring an expense, or revenue account up to its true balance in an attempt to match earned revenue and incurred expenses (in an accrual system).

18. A_____ postpones the recognition or sale (although you have received the money) until you earn it.

21. The_____ of sales or revenue in an accrual basis system result when sales are not earned.

23. Accrued _____ _____ tries to show the true interest expense in a year although payment is not yet due.

Down:

1. The allowance method of bad debt tries to estimate the bad debt expense in the old year when the sales were made, in an attempt to arrive at a true picture of_____ _____ .

2. The _____ _____ of accounting uses the matching concept.

3. A_____ is a sale, when it is earned whether or not money is received under the accrual basis of accounting.

5. The normal balance of accrued revenue is a _____(abbreviation).

9. Unearned revenue is_____ revenue.

10. Under an accrual basis_____ is earned.

11. _____ result in a cash basis system when they are paid.

15. Usually unearned revenue has a_____ balance.

226

19. Another name for a sale is _____ .

20. The _____ basis of accounting matches earned revenue and incurred expenses.

22. A _____ (abbreviation) to an expense increases it.

5. Depreciation

Across:

1. Declining-balance and sum-of-the-year's digits result in _____ depreciation compared to the straight-line method.
6. Cost of equipment — accumulated depreciation = book _____ .
7. _____ of production estimates depreciation based on the output of the machine.
9. Straight-_____ method of depreciation spreads the depreciation expense equally over the life estimation of the asset.
10. The "_____" method of depreciation is based on a fractional basis (sum of number of years to be depreciated = denominator and years left to be depreciated is the numerator).
15. Sum-of-the-year's digit is _____ to declining-balance in using accelerated depreciation.
16. Equipment is an _____ .
17. Straight-line spreads an _____ (equal) amount of depreciation expense over a number of years.

Down:

2. Accumulated depreciation is a _____ _____ .
3. Depreciation is the wearing out or the spreading out of the original cost of the assets through use and/or the passing of _____ .
4. The wearing out or spreading out the original cost of an asset over time, or through use is called _____ .
5. The _____ -balance method accelerates the rate of depreciation.
7. Units of production looks at the _____ of the machine.
8. Another name for trade-in value is _____ value.
11. Usually _____ value is not used in declining-balance method. (Except possibiy in later years).
12. Declining-balance is usually _____ the straight-line rate.
13. In calculating depreciation in double declining-balance method of depreciation the book value _____ is calculated by equipment-accumulated depreciation.
14. Depreciation expense is a paper entry which increases a company's _____ or expenses, as the original cost of certain assets (equip) are spread through use and/or the passing of time.

6. Notes and Interest

Across:

1. Written promise which states someone owes us some money is called a
   _____ _____ .

5. Maturity value of a note — discount taken by a bank on the note = the persons or companies _____ .

8. The person or company who received money from a promissory note is called the _____ .

9. The person or company who promises to pay money involving a promissory _____ .

12. A person or company who exchanges a note for cash to a bank (before maturity value) is said to have had the note _____ .

13. A note is _____ when the failure or refusal of a person to pay a note that is due.

14. The _____ _____ is the % rate that a bank uses in discounting a note. (maturity $\frac{\text{value X \% X \# of days}}{360}$ bank must wait for note to become due)

Down:

1. The account called _____ _____ shows a definite written promise which states the amount we owe someone.

2. The cost of using someone else's money is called _____ .

3. Thirty days has Sept., April, June and November; all the rest have 31 except February, which has 28, and 29 during leap year is a __ __ __ __ __ .

4. Interest earned on a note is a form of _____ .

5. _____ + interest = maturity value.

6. _____ _____ 60-day method is a shortcut method of calculating interest.

7. _____ _____ = principal + interest.

10. The cost of borrowing money is an _____ .

11. The time when a note reaches maturity is called its _____ _____ .

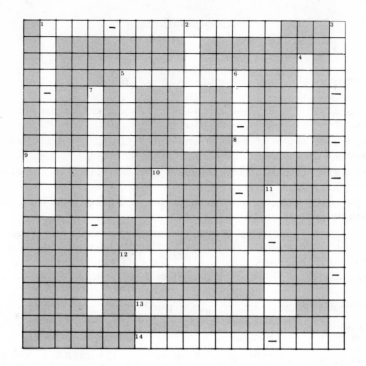

7. Corporations

Across:

1. Three types of business organization are sole proprietorships, partnerships and _____ .

5. _____ certificates show or verify the amount of ownership and rights of a stockholder in a corporation.

9. The normal balance of retained earnings is a _____ (use abbreviation).

10. The normal balance of treasury stock is a _____ (use abbreviation).

12. Common stock subscriptions receivable has a normal balance of a _____ (use abbreviation).

15. _____ earnings is that portion of profits of a corporation that are kept in the business which have been accumulating or building up in a business over the years.

16. _____ is an estimated value of the rights of the owners to a single share of stock in a corporation.

17. Stockholder's _____ = paid-in capital plus retained earnings.

20. _____ on stock results when selling stock (or issuing stock) at a price that is greater than par value.

21. _____ preferred stock usually gives the investor a definite or certain amount of dividends each year.

Down:

1. _____ _____ certificate is one type of stock which shows the amount of ownership and rights one has in a corporation.

2. Cummulative type of dividends usually deal with _____ stock.

3. Stock certificates show the _____ and ownership one has in a corporation.

4. Contributed capital plus retained earnings = _____ equity.

5. A _____ _____ is usually used by a corporation to reduce the market price of their common stock.

6. The _____ section of a sole proprietorship can be compared to the stockholder's equity section of a corporation.

7. _____ stock is a contra equity account.

8. The _____ _____ of stock has no relation to its par value.

11. The _____ right allows a stockholder the opportunity to buy more and more stock in order to keep his same fractional amount interest or rights in the corporation.

13. _____ on stocks result when selling stocks (or issuing stocks) at a price that is less than par value.

14. A _____ dividend results in no cash being given to the stockholder.

16. Another way of raising finances for a firm may be to sell _____.

18. Each state has its own requirements for _____ capital.

19. A _____ (abbreviation) reduces retained earnings.

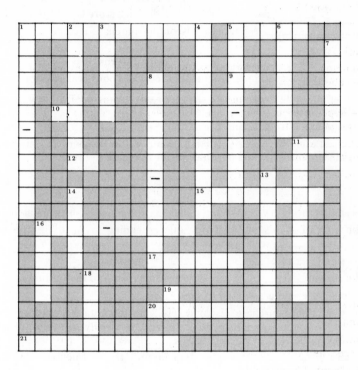

8. Merchandise Co.
(cost of goods sold)

Across:

1. Beginning Merchandise _____ is an asset with a debit balance on the balance sheet.

4. _____ inventory reduces the total cost of the goods sold.

8. _____ assumes old merchandise in a store is sold before the new.

10. _____ —purchase discounts—purchase returns equals net purchases.

12. Sales — sales _____ — sales returns = net sales.

13. _____ inventory and net purchases = cost of goods available for sale.

14. Net sales assumes all _____ _____ have been subtracted from gross sales.

16. Gross sales — (returns and discounts) = _____ _____ .

18. Received a credit _____ from Ralph Brothers for defective merchandise (debit accounts payable—credit purchase return).

Down:

1. As ending inventory is overstated, net _____ is overstated.

2. The cost of goods available for sale — ending inventory = the cost of _____ sold.

3. Net sales — _____ _____ = gross profit.

6. The cost of _____ sold is an expense to the business.

7. Merchandise sold is assumed to be a _____ .

9. Sales discount, purchase discount, etc., are temporary accounts which are closed to _____ _____ and eventually to capital or retained earnings.

10. _____ inventory system doesn't try to calculate cost of each good sold at time of sale.

11. Gross profit — operating _____ = net income.

15. Purchase _____ reduce the cost of purchasing.

17. _____ assumes new merchandise in a store is sold before the old.

9. Voucher System

Across:

1. In a voucher system the _____ _____ takes the place of the cash payments journal.
4. A debit to vouchers payable will _____ what is owed.
6. A _____ to purchases results in an increase.
7. Recording purchases at net assumes the _____ will be taken.
9. A voucher contains information about a _____ or obligation that is to be paid.
13. The _____ contains information about an obligation that is to be paid.
15. The _____ _____ journal is not used in a voucher system.
16. The term accounts payable is replaced by voucher _____ in a voucher system.
17. A voucher is sometimes attached to a _____ .
19. The _____ of a voucher pays the payee.
20. In a voucher system, the voucher register takes the place of the purchase _____ .
22. Recording purchase at _____ will not show discounts that have been lost.
23. The voucher system is an internal type of control _____ .
24. An account called discount lost relates to discounts that were not _____.

Down:

1. Vouchers payable normally has a _____ balance.
2. The check _____ is used to pay bills in a voucher system.
3. A voucher file may take the place of a _____ ledger.
5. Purchase normally has a _____ balance. (use abbreviation)
8. A check register is a special _____ .
10. A voucher is assigned a voucher _____ .
11. The voucher system is a way of controlling _____ .
12. The _____ journal is replaced by the voucher register in a voucher system.
14. The _____ of the check written in the check register is posted to the voucher register.

236

16. The receiver of money from an obligation is called the _____ .
18. When recording purchases at net discounts are almost _____ tried to be taken.
21. The _____ amount of recording purchases is the opposite of using the gross amount.

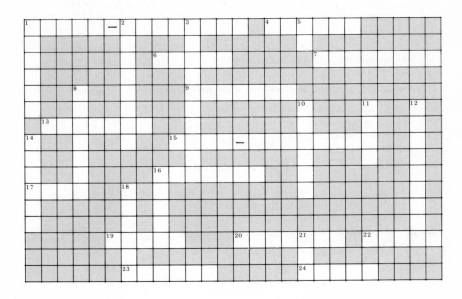

10. Accounting I, II Mix

Across:

3. Accounts _____ is a liability account that indicates that we owe someone some money for merchandise or services obtained.

7. _____ _____ bring up to date certain balances in the ledger accounts at the end of an accounting period to their correct or true balance.

8. _____ payable is a *written promise* which states the amount we owe someone. It is a liability account.

10. The _____ _____ for bad debts matches bad debt expenses to the period of time that the sales were earned or recognized.

13. _____ stands for End of Month.

14. Sales usually have a _____ balance.

16. _____ debts is an expense that results when a customer does not pay his bill for goods or services that were charged to his account.

18. A = L & OE = The accounting _____ .

23. _____ reconciliations help to prove the accuracy of the customer's records versus the records of the bank.

24. Allowance for doubtful accounts is a _____ asset.

26. The _____ inventory of a merchandise company on December 31, becomes the beginning inventory on January 1.

27. _____ _____ summarize the effects of temporary accounts on capital or owner equity.

29. Gross pay — deductions = _____ pay.

31. 2/15, n/60 means that a _____ discount of 2% will result if the bill is paid within 15 days.

35. Another name for a cash payments journal is called _____ _____ journal.

36. _____ revenue means that sales have been earned but have not been recorded, nor has money yet been received.

37. Pencil _____ helps to summarize the debits and credits of an account in order to get a new balance.

38. _____ profit is net sales minus cost of goods sold.

39. _____ is the rights of others to things (assets) owned by a business.

41. Accumulated depreciation is a _____ account.

42. Assets — liabilities = _____ .

43. Accounts payable, notes payable, bonds payable are examples of _____ .

44. _____ entries bring up to date the trial balance.

46. A cash _____ was declared by the board of directors of Y corporation.

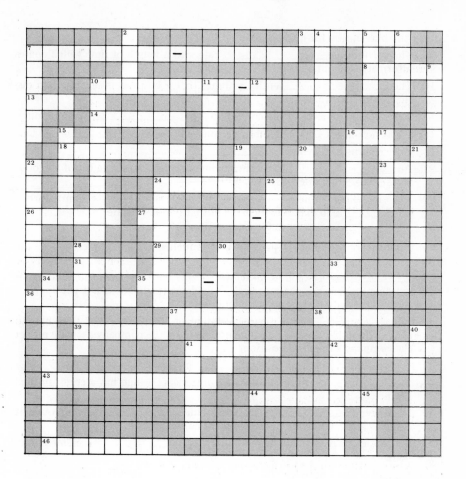

Down:

2. An invoice is sometimes called a _____ when purchasing goods or services.

4. The T- _____ is used mainly for demonstration purposes.

5. _____ discount results when the borrower does not receive the full amount of the loan.

6. A journal _____ records transactions or happenings in a business.

7. Cash, accounts, receivable, prepaid rent are examples of _____.

9. A premium on _____ results when the sales price is greater than par value.

10. The _____ equation is A = L & OE.

11. Interest payable, accounts payable, salaries payable may be examples _____ liabilities.

239

12. An abbreviation for merchandise.

15. The accounting _____ refers to a length of time which relates information about a business.

16. The _____ entity assumes that a business is separate and distinct from its owners.

17. The opposite of a credit memorandum is a _____ memorandum.

19. Abbreviation for Certified Public Accountant is_____.

20. Sales returns usually has a _____ balance.

21. An _____ is another name for a bill showing a list of all goods and service bought or sold.

22. The matching principle compares (under the accrual system) earned _____ to expenses incurred in that period of time.

24. Payroll is based on a _____ year.

25. Payment of a vouchers payable in a voucher system is recorded in the _____ register.

28. _____ expenses deal with expenses that are accumulating or building up that are not recorded or paid for (payment is not yet due) but really represent an expense in the old year.

30. The _____ of financial statements by independent films help to assure the public that the statements made by the company actually reflect the company's financial position.

33. Straight-line is a type of _____ method.

34. _____ depreciation is a contra asset which has a credit normal balance.

40. Employer's _____ taxes include FICA, federal unemployment compensation; and state unemployment compensation.

41. The opposite of a debit memorandum is a _____ memorandum.

45. The opposite of notes payable is _____ receivable.

11. Accounting Hunt

Words run in all directions—forward, backward, up, down and diagonally.

Find in the diagram either the word to fill in the blank in the sentence or the word to describe the sentence.

There are 16 words to be found. Words run in *all* directions.

```
A  R  T  N  O  C  B  E  U  P  V
C  T  N  U  O  C  C  A  S  O  J
L  J  M  I  Y  V  S  W  N  D  L
A  S  T  C  I  O  R  P  M  K  E
N  A  L  I  L  O  T  S  O  C  Z
R  E  E  N  B  S  R  W  R  Q  R
U  L  W  A  F  E  E  E  L  M  E
O  F  I  F  A  C  D  S  G  Q  T
J  G  F  N  H  I  M  S  Q  L  A
B  B  A  E  T  A  D  X  J  O  L
J  O  F  Z  C  J  E  D  I  L  S
L  A  T  I  P  A  C  S  A  M  J
```

1. Author of "Don't Lose Your Balance"?

2. What is the word for an error in writing a number?

3. The first columns in a journal are for the transaction _____?

4. When a bank collects on a note receivable it will deduct from the amount collected a _____?

5. The life of a business is divided into accounting periods; and each period is a recurring accounting _____?

6. Give the first letters that represent the accounting function that the first goods brought into a store will be the first goods sold (for a merchandise company).

7. What is the name given to the left side of any account (or a number entered on the left side)?

8. What is the word describing the rights of the owner to things (assets or properties) owned by a business.

9. Name the book or place where transactions are *first* put or recorded.

10. What is the name given to the right side of any account (or a number entered on the right side)?

11. The beginning inventory plus purchases less ending inventory equals the _____ of goods sold.

12. What is the transaction called when money is allowed to be used by an individual or firm by a bank?

13. What is referred to as a device or place which records and summarizes the increase or decrease of an individual _____?

14. Name of an institution where an individual or firm can borrow money with interest.

15. The relation of a company's current assets to its current liabilities is known as it current _____ .

16. Accumulated depreciation and allowance for doubtful accounts are referred to as _____ accounts.

Answer Sheet

Answers to: 1. Rule of Debits and Credits, Categories and Normal Balances

Across: (2) debit; (3) accumulated; (7) asset; (8) credit; (9) capital; (14) expense; (16) increase; (17) liability; (19) increase; (21) expense; (22) prepaid; (24) debit; (26) account; (29) DR.; (30) increase; (31) debit; (32) cash; (33) asset; (34) account.

Down: (1) decreased; (2) debit; (4) usual; (5) liability; (6) usual; (10) retained; (11) debit; (12) decrease; (13) debit; (15) debit; (18) debit; (20) expenses; (23) debit; (25) expense; (26) asset; (27) contra; (28) credit; (29) debit;

Answers to: 2. Adjusting and Closing Entries

Across: (1) withdrawals; (6) liab; (7) depreciation; (9) asset; (10) prepaid asset; (12) net income; (14) expense; (16) normal; (17) revenue; (19) net loss; (22) loss; (24) revenue; (25) liab; (26) unearned; (27) year end closing.

Down: (2) revenue; (3) asset; (4) capital; (5) drawings; (7) deficit; (8) accrued expense; (11) expenses; (13) income; (15) drawing; (18) normal; (20) expense; (21) summary; (23) sumary.

Answers to: 3. Journals

Across: (1) special; (5) folio; (8) cash payments; (9) ledger; (10) sales; (11) accounts; (13) sales—returns; (14) posting; (15) purchase returns; (17) disbursement; (18) subsidiary.

Down: (2) purchase; (3) slide; (4) journals; (6) cash receipts; (7) general; (12) schedule; (16) sundry.

Answers to: 4. **Accruals and Deferrals**

Across: (2) cash basis; (4) liability; (6) revenue; (7) received; (8) matching principle; (12) debit; (13) expense; (14) paid; (16) incurred; (17) entry; (18) deferral; (21) postponing; (23) interest expense.

Down: (1) net income; (2) accrual basis; (3) sale; (5) cr; (9) not; (10) revenue; (11) expenses; (15) credit; (19) revenue; (20) accrual; (22) dr.

Answers to: 5. **Depreciation**

Across: (1) accelerated; (6) value; (7) units; (9) line; (10) digit; (15) similar; (16) asset; (17) even.

Down: (2) contra asset; (3) time; (4) depreciation; (5) declining; (7) use; (8) residual; (11) salvage; (12) twice; (13) balance; (14) cost.

Answers to: 6. **Notes and Interest**

Across: (1) note receivable; (5) proceeds; (8) payee; (9) maker; (12) discounted; (13) dishonored; (14) discount rate.

Down: (1) note payable; (2) interest; (3) days in a month rule; (4) income; (5) principal; (6) six per cent; (7) maturity value; (10) expense; (11) due date.

Answers to: 7. **Corporations**

Across: (1) corporations; (5) stock; (9) cr; (10) dr; (12) dr; (15) retained; (16) book value; (17) equity; (20) premiums; (21) cumulative.

Down: (1) common stock; (2) preferred; (3) rights; (4) shareholders; (5) stock split; (6) capital; (7) treasury; (8) market value; (11) preemptive; (13) discounts; (14) stock; (16) bonds; (18) legal; (19) dr.

Answers to: 8. Merchandise Co.

Across: (1) inventory; (4) ending; (8) FIFO; (10) purchases; (12) discounts; (13) beginning; (14) sales returns; (16) net sales; (18) memorandum.

Down: (1) income; (2) merchandise; (3) cost of goods sold; (6) goods; (7) cost; (9) income summary; (10) periodic; (11) expense; (15) returns; (17) LIFO.

Answers to: 9. Voucher System

Across: (1) check register; (4) reduce; (6) debit; (7) discount; (9) invoice; (13) voucher; (15) cash payments (16) payable; (17) bill; (19) payer; (20) journal; (22) gross; (23) system; (24) taken.

Down: (1) credit; (2) register; (3) subsidiary; (5) dr; (8) journal; (10) number; (11) cash; (12) purchase; (14) number; (16) payee; (18) always; (21) net.

Answers to: 10. Accounting I, II Mix

Across: (3) payable; (7) adjusting entries; (8) notes; (10) allowance method; (13) eom; (14) credit; (16) bad; (18) equation; (23) bank; (24) contra; (26) ending; (27) closing entries; (29) net; (31) cash; (35) cash disbursement; (36) accrued; (37) footing; (38) gross; (39) equity; (41) contra; (42) capital; (43) liabilities; (44) adjusting; (46) dividend.

Down: (2) bill; (4) account; (5) bank; (6) entry; (7) assets; (9) stock; (10) accounting; (11) current; (12) mdse; (15) period; (16) business; (17) debit; (19) CPA; (20) debit; (21) invoice; (22) revenue; (24) calendar; (25) check; (28) accrued; (30) auditing; (33) depreciation; (34) accumulated; (40) payroll; (41) credit; (45) notes.

Answers to: 11. Accounting Hunt

(1) Slater; (2) slide; (3) date; (4) fee; (5) cycle; (6) FIFO; (7) debit; (8) capital; (9) journal; (10) credit; (11) cost; (12) loan; (13) account; (14) bank; (15) ratio; (16) contra.

Appendix I Accounting: Common Formulas and Equations

1. Assets = Liabilities + Owner Equity (Capital)
2. Assets = Liabilities + Owner's Equity + Revenues — Expenses — Drawing
3. Liabilities = Assets — Owner's Equity
4. Owner's Equity = Assets — Liabilities
5. Income Statement

Revenues
— Expenses
= Net Income

6. Balance Sheet

Assets = Liabilities
+ Owner's Equity

7. Statement of Change in Owner's Equity

Beginning Capital + Net Income — Drawings = Ending Capital

8. Assets = Liabilities + Owner's Equity + Revenues — Expenses — Drawings

Dr.	Cr.	Dr.	Cr.	Dr.	Cr.	Dr.	Cr.	Dr.	Cr.	Dr.	Cr.
+	—	—	+	—		+		—	+	+	—			+	—

9. Trial Balance =

Debits	Credits
Assets	Liabilities
+ Expenses	+ Owner's Equity
+ Drawings	+ Revenue

10. *Adjustments*

    Beginning Supplies — Supplies used up = Supplies on hand.

    Prepaid Rent — Amount expired = Amount of Rent paid in advance remaining.

    Equipment* — Accumulated Depreciation = Amount of Depreciation not taken as yet on the equipment.

*This is historical cost and will not change.

	Debits	Credits
11. The Adjusted Trial Balance on a work sheet	Assets + Expenses + Drawings	Liabilities + Owner's Equity + Revenue + Accumulated Depreciation

	Debits	Credits
12. Income Statement Columns on a work sheet	Expenses Net Income	Revenues

	Debit	Credit
13. Balance Sheet Column on a Work Sheet	Assets + Drawings	Liabilities + Accumulated Depreciation + Capital + Net Income

		Debit	Credit
14. Post Closing Trial Balance All temporary accounts in ledger were cleared to zero by closing entries	=	Assets	Liabilities Owner's Equity (new)

FOR A MERCHANDISE COMPANY

15.

Sales Returns and Allowances		Sales Discount		Purchases	
Dr.	Cr.	Dr.	Cr.	Dr.	Cr.
+	−	+	− ,	+	−

Purchases Returns and Allowances		Purchases Discount		Freight	
Dr.	Cr.	Dr.	Cr.	Dr.	Cr.
−	+	−	+	+	−

Merchandise Inventory	
Dr.	Cr.
+	−

16. Issuing a Credit Memo 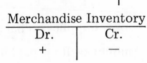 Accounts Receivable (−)
or receiving a Debit Memo ➤ Sales Returns and Allowance (+)

17. Unearned Revenue

Dr.	Cr.
−	+

This is a liability.

18. Sales − Sales Returns and Allowances − Sales Discount = Net Sales

19. Net Purchases = Purchases − Purchase Discount − Purchase Ret. and Allow.

20a. Cost of goods purchased = Net Purchases + Freight

20. Merchandise (goods) Available for Sale = Beginning Inventory + Cost of Goods Purchased

21. Cost of Goods Sold = Goods available for sale − Ending Inventory

22. Gross Profit = Net Sales − Cost of Goods Sold.

23. Net Income = Gross Profit − Operating Expenses.

24. Bank Reconcilation

Bank	*Book*
+ Deposits In transit	− Service Charge Collection Charge
− Checks Outstanding	− Not Sufficient Funds
+ − Bank errors	+ Note Collected
	+ − Errors in recording checks, etc.

25. FICA Tax Payable

Dr.	Cr.
−	+

State Unemployment Tax Payable

Dr.	Cr.
−	+

Federal Unemployment

Dr.	Cr.
−	+

Payroll Tax Expenses

Dr.	Cr.
+	−

26. Petty Cash

Dr.	Cr.
+	−

27. Vouchers Payable

Dr.	Cr.
−	+

Discount Lost

Dr.	Cr.
+	−

28. Interest = Principal × Rate × Time

29. Maturity Value = Face Value of Note + Interest on Note

30. Discount on a Note = Maturity Value × $\dfrac{\text{No. of Days Bank Holds Note}}{36}$ × Discount Rate

31. Proceeds = Maturity Value − Discount on a Note

32. 6% 60 on 500. = $5.00

33.

Bad Debt Expense		Allowance for Doubtful Accounts	
Dr.	Cr.	Dr.	Cr.
+	−	−	+

34.   Accounts Receivable
− Allowance for Doubtful Accounts

= Relizable Accounts Receivable

35. Weighted Average Cost per Unit = $\dfrac{\text{\# of Units} \times \text{Unit Price (Total Cost)}}{\text{Total \# of Units}}$

36. Average Cost per Unit × # of Units in Inventory = Value of Ending Inventory.

37.

	Overstated	Understated
If Beginning Inventory	Net Income is Understated	Net Income is Overstated
Ending Inventory	Net Income is Overstated	Net Income is Understated

If Ending Inventory is Overstated Cost of Goods sold will be Understated and thus Gross Profit as well as Net Income will be Overstated.

38. Beginning Inventory + Net Purchases + Additional Mark Ups = Merchandise Available for Sale.

39. Retail Value of Goods Available for Sale − Net Sales − Mark Downs = Retail Value of Ending Inventory.

40. $\dfrac{1}{\text{\# of Years to be Depreciated (Useful Life)}}$ = Annual Rate of Depreciation

41. Straight Line Depreciation = $\dfrac{\text{Cost} - \text{Salvage}}{\text{Useful Life (years)}}$

42. Units of Production = $\dfrac{\text{Cost} - \text{Salvage}}{\text{est. units of production}}$

43. Book Value = Cost − Accumulated Depreciation.

44. Declining Balance
    (Double)

Book Value (Beginning of Year) $\times$ Rate (Twice Straight Line)

45. Sum of Years

$$\left(\frac{\text{reverse order of years}}{\frac{N(N+1)}{2}}\right) \times \left(\begin{array}{c}\text{Cost}\\-\ \text{Salvage}\end{array}\right)$$

46. If Book Value = Trade-In: No gain or loss
    If Book Value greater than Trade-In: Loss
    If Book Value less than Trade-In: Gain

47.

Stockholder's Equity		Preferred Stock		Prem. on Stock	
Dr.	Cr.	Dr.	Cr.	Dr.	Cr.
—	+	—	+	—	+

Common Stock		Discount on Common Stock		Retained Earnings	
Dr.	Cr.	Dr.	Cr.	Dr.	Cr.
—	+	+	—	—	+

48.

Subscriptions Receivable		Common Stock Subscriptions	
Dr.	Cr.	Dr.	Cr.
+	—	—	+

Paid in Capital		Treasury Stock		Retained Earnings Appropriated	
Dr.	Cr.	Dr.	Cr.	Dr.	Cr.
—	+	+	—	—	+

49. Revenue — Cost of Goods Sold = Gross Profit — Direct Departmental expenses = Contribution Margin — Indirect expenses = Net Income from Operations.

Appendix II Review of Accounting I and II

REVIEW OF ACCOUNTING I AND II

Area of Coverage in Text	The Situation	Typical Accounts Affected	Category	Rules	Sample Journal Entry That Would Result
Accounting cycle for a service company (transactions)	John Smith invested $10,000 into the Real Estate Agency	Cash J. Smith, Capital	Asset Owner's Equity	Dr. ↑ Cr. ↑	Cash 10,000 J. Smith, Capital 10,000
	Paid 2 months rent in advance $500	Prepaid Rent Cash	Asset Asset	Dr. ↑ Cr. ↓	Prepaid Rent 500 Cash 500
	Bought office equipment for cash—$300	Office Equipment Cash	Asset Asset	Dr. ↑ Cr. ↓	Office Equipment 300 Cash 300
	Bought office supplies on account for $100	Office Supplies Accounts Payable	Asset Liability	Dr. ↑ Cr. ↑	Office Supplies 100 Accounts Payable 100
	Sold a home and *received* a $500 commission in cash	Cash Commissions Earned	Asset Revenue	Dr. ↑ Cr. ↑	Cash 500 Commissions Earned 500
	Sold a home and will receive a $1,000 commission next month	Accounts Receivable Commissions Earned	Asset Revenue	Dr. ↑ Cr. ↑	Accounts Receivable 1,000 Commissions Earned 1,000
	Commissions previously earned were received—$1,000	Cash Accounts Receivable	Asset Asset	Dr. ↑ Cr. ↓	Cash 1,000 Accounts Receivable 1,000
	Bought equipment for $500 paying $60 in cash and charging the balance	Equipment Accounts Payable Cash	Asset Liability Asset	Dr. ↑ Cr. ↑ Cr. ↓	Equipment 500 Accounts Payable 440 Cash 60
	Agreed to manage a condominium and collected $3,000 in advance	Cash Unearned Management Fees	Asset Liability	Dr. ↑ Cr. ↑	Cash 3,000 Unearned Man. Fees 3,000
	Paid balance owed $440 on equipment previously bought on account	Accounts Payable Cash	Liability Asset	Dr. ↓ Cr. ↓	Accounts Payable 440 Cash 440
	Paid secretary salary $100	Salary Expense Cash	Expense Asset	Dr. ↑ Cr. ↓	Salary Expense 100 Cash 100
	John Smith withdrew $50 from the Business	J. Smith, Withdrawal Cash	Drawing (OE) Asset	Dr. ↑ Cr. ↓	J. Smith, Withdrawal 50 Cash 50

Area of Coverage in Text	The Situation	Typical Accounts Affected	Category	Rules	Sample Journal Entry That Would Result	
Adjusting Entries	Rent expired—$200	Rent Expense Prepaid Rent	Expense Asset	Dr. ↑ Cr. →	Rent Expense Prepaid Rent	200 200
	Supplies *Used Up*—$150	Supplies Expense Supplies	Expense Asset	Dr. ↑ Cr. →	Supplies Expense Supplies	150 150
	Equipment depreciates $100	Depreciation Exp. Accumulated Depr.	Expense Contra Asset	Dr. ↑ Cr. ↑	Depreciation Exp. Equip. Accum. Depr. Equip.	100 100
	Accrued Salaries $50	Salary Expense Salaries Payable	Expense Liability	Dr. ↑ Cr. ↑	Salaries Expense Salaries Payable	50 50
	Unearned Revenue now earned $1,000	Unearned Revenue Earned Revenue	Liability Revenue	Dr. → Cr. ↑	Unearned Revenue Earned Revenue	1,000 1,000
Closing Entries	Closed Fees Earned balance into Income Summary (expense and revenue summary) $1,000	Fees Earned Income Summary	Revenue Owner's Equity	Dr. → Cr. —	Fees Earned Income Summary	1,000 1,000
	Closed heat ($50), telephone ($100), and wages ($500) to Income Summary	Income Summary Heat Expense Telephone Expense Wage Expense	Owner's Equity Expense Expense Expense	Dr. — Cr. → Cr. → Cr. →	Income Summary Heat Expense Telephone Expense Wage Expense	650 50 100 500
	Close balance in Income Summary to John Smith Capital	Income Summary J. Smith, Capital	Owner's Equity Owner's Equity	Dr. — Cr. ↑	Income Summary J. Smith, Capital	350 350
	Closed $50 in Withdrawal Account	J. Smith, Capital J. Smith, Drawing	Owner's Equity Owner's Equity	Dr. → Cr. ↑	J. Smith Capital J. Smith, Drawing	50 50
Accounting for a Merchandise Company	Sold merchandise on credit $5,000	Accounts Receivable Sales	Asset Revenue	Dr. ↑ Cr. ↑	Accounts Receivable Sales	5,000 5,000
	Customer returned unsatisfactory merchandise $150 (issued credit memo and received a debit memo)	Sales Returns and Allowances Accounts Receivable	Contra Revenue Asset	Dr. ↑ Cr. →	Sales Returns and Allowances Accounts Receivable-xxx	150 150
	Sold merchandise on credit $2,000 and sales tax of $100	Accounts Receivable Sales Sales Tax Payable	Asset Revenue Liability	Dr. ↑ Cr. ↑ Cr. ↑	Accounts Receivable Sales Sales Tax Payable	2,100 2,000 100

Area of Coverage in Text	The Situation	Typical Accounts Affected	Category	Rules	Sample Journal Entry That Would Result
	Received payment from past sale less discount. ($100 — $2 discount)	Cash Sales Discount Accounts Receivable	Asset Contra Revenue Asset	Dr. ↑ Dr. ↑ Cr. →	Cash 98 Sales Discount 2 Accounts Receivable 100
	Purchased merchandise on credit $1,000	Purchases Accounts Payable	Cost of Goods Sold Liability	Dr. ↑ Cr. ↑	Purchases 1,000 Accounts Payable 1,000
	Paid for previous purchase $980 ($1,000 less 2% discount)	Accounts Payable Purchase Discounts Cash	Liability Contra Cost of Goods Sold Asset	Dr. → Cr. ↑ Cr. →	Accounts Payable 1,000 Purchase Discounts 20 Cash 980
	Returned defective goods $50 (issued a debit memo and received a credit memo)	Accounts Payable Purchase Returns and Allowances	Liability Contra Cost of Goods Sold	Dr. → Cr. ↑	Accounts Payable 50 Purchase Returns and Allowances 50
	Paid freight charge on goods $10	Freight-In Cash	Cost of Goods Sold Asset	Dr. ↑ Cr. →	Freight-In 10 Cash 10
Voucher System	Purchased merchandise $2,000 (gross)	Purchases Vouchers Payable	Cost of Goods Sold Liability	Dr. ↑ Cr. ↑	Purchases 2,000 Vouchers Payable 2,000
	Paid for merchandise $1,960 ($2,000 — $40 discount)	Vouchers Payable Purchase Discount Cash	Liability Contra Cost of Goods Sold Asset	Dr. → Cr. ↑ Cr. →	Vouchers Payable 2,000 Purchase Discount 40 Cash 1,960
	Purchased $2,000 of merchandise (recorded at net 2% discount)	Purchases Vouchers Payable	Cost of Goods Sold Liability	Dr. ↑ Cr. ↑	Purchases 1,960 Vouchers Payable 1,960
	Lost discount on purchase recorded at net $40	Discount Lost Vouchers Payable	Owner's Equity Liability	Dr. ↑ Cr. ↑	Discount Lost 40 Vouchers Payable 40
	Returned defective merchandise $200—received a credit memo	Voucher Payable Purchase Returns and Allowances	Liability Contra Cost of Goods Sold	Dr. → Cr. ↑	Vouchers Payable 200 Purchase Returns and Allowances 200
Petty Cash	Established Petty Cash $50 Check #10	Petty Cash Cash	Asset Asset	Dr. ↑ Cr. →	Petty Cash 50 Cash 50

Area of Coverage in Text	The Situation	Typical Accounts Affected	Category	Rules	Sample Journal Entry That Would Result	
	Replenished Petty Cash for $5 bandaids, $15 postage, $10 cleaning, Check #15	Bandaids Postage Cleaning Cash	Expense Expense Expense Asset	Dr. ← Dr. ← Dr. ← Cr. →	Bandaids Expense Postage Expense Cleaning Expense Cash	5 15 10 30
	During month paid $2 for postage from petty cash	NO ENTRY IS NEEDED AUXILIARY PETTY CASH RECORD COULD BE UPDATED				
	Cash sales today $100 with shortage of $2 (tape more than cash)	Cash Cash Over and Short Sales	Asset Expense Revenue	Dr. ← Dr. ← Cr. →	Cash Cash Over and Short Sales	98 2 100
	Cash sales $100 with overage of $4 (tape less than cash)	Cash Cash Over and Short Sales	Asset Revenue Revenue	Dr. ← Cr. ← Cr. ←	Cash Cash Over and Short Sales	104 4 100
Bank Reconciliation	Recorded note collection by bank $200 less a collection expense of $5	Cash Collection Expense Notes Receivable	Asset Expense Asset	Dr. ← Dr. ← Cr. →	Cash Collection Expense Notes Receivable	195 5 200
	Record NSF of $1,000 to charge back John Bill	Accounts Receivable Cash	Asset Asset	Dr. ← Cr. →	Accounts Receivable— J. Bill Cash	1,000 1,000
	Record $5 bank service charge	Miscellaneous Exp. Cash	Expense Asset	Dr. ← Cr. →	Miscellaneous Expense Cash	5 5
Accounts Receivables (Bad Debts)	Recorded estimated $2,000 in bad debts utilizing the allowance method	Bad Debts Expense Allow. for Doubtful Accounts	Expense Contra Asset	Dr. ← Cr. ←	Bad Debts Expense Allow. Doubtful Acct.	2,000 2,000
	Wrote off uncollectable account of George Marcus $200 utilizing the allowance method	Allowance for doubtful accounts Accounts Receivable	Contra Asset Asset	Dr. → Cr. →	Allow. Doubtful Acct. Accounts Receivable— G. Marcus	200 200
	A/ Reinstated account of George Marcus and B/ received payment in full of $200	Accounts Receivable Allowance for Doubtful Accounts Cash Accounts Receivable	Asset Contra Asset Asset Asset	Dr. ← Cr. ← Dr. ← Cr. →	Accounts Receivable Allow. Doubtful Acct. Cash Accounts Receivable	200 200 200 200

Area of Coverage in Text	The Situation	Typical Accounts Affected	Category	Rules		Sample Journal Entry That Would Result	
Direct Method	Wrote off George Marcus $200 as an uncollectable account	Bad Debt Expense	Expense	Dr.	←	Bad Debt Expense	200	
		Accounts Receivable	Asset	Cr.	→	Accounts Receivable		200
Notes and Interest	Bought store equipment with a one year 8% note—$2,000	Store Equipment	Asset	Dr.	←	Store Equipment	2,000	
		Notes Payable	Liability	Cr.	←	Notes Payable		2,000
	Gave a 90 day 6% note in settlement of Account Payable $500	Accounts Payable	Liability	Dr.	→	Accounts Payable	500	
		Notes Payable	Liability	Cr.	←	Notes Payable		500
	Bill Flynn pd. interest bearing note $550 (principal was $520-interest $30)	Notes Payable	Liability	Dr.	→	Notes Payable	520	
		Interest Expense	Expense	Dr.	←	Interest Expense	30	
		Cash	Asset	Cr.	→	Cash		550
	Moe Black discounted a $2,000 note at 10%	Cash	Asset	Dr.	←	Cash	1,800	
		Interest Expense	Expense	Dr.	←	Interest Expense	200	
		Notes Payable	Liability	Cr.	←	Notes Payable		2,000
	Moe Black paid back previous loan that was discounted	Notes Payable	Liability	Dr.	→	Notes Payable	1,000	
		Cash	Asset	Cr.	→	Cash		1,000
	Collected a note $1,000 with interested earned $50	Cash	Asset	Dr.	←	Cash	1,050	
		Notes Receivable	Asset	Cr.	→	Notes Receivable		1,000
		Interest Earned	Revenue (other inc.)	Cr.	←	Interest Earned		50
	Charged Sheldon Brown's account for his dishonored $600 6% 60 day note	Accounts Receivable	Asset	Dr.	←	Accounts Receivable	606	
		Interest Earned	Revenue (other inc.)	Cr.	←	Interest Earned		6
		Notes Receivable	Assets	Cr.	→	Notes Receivable		600
	Discounted Irene Westings's note ($1,000) at First Bank—Proceeds $990	Cash	Asset	Dr.	←	Cash	990	
		Interest Expense	Expense	Dr.	←	Interest Expense	10	
		Notes Receivable	Asset	Cr.	→	Notes Receivable*		1,000
	Discounted Shari Walker's note ($2,000) at Last Bank—Proceeds $2,010	Cash	Asset	Dr.	←	Cash	2,010	
		Interest Earned	Revenue (other inc.)	Cr.	←	Interest Earned	10	
		Notes Receivable	Asset	Cr.	→	Notes Receivable		2,000
	Irene Westing's account is charged for dishonored note plus a protest fee of $5	Accounts Receivable	Asset	Dr.	←	Accounts Receivable	1,005	
		Cash	Asset	Cr.	→	Cash		1,005

*Some texts use Notes Receivable Discounted.

Area of Coverage in Text	The Situation	Typical Accounts Affected	Category	Rules	Sample Journal Entry That Would Result
Inventory	Interest accrued on a note $5 by year end	Interest Receivable Interest Earned	Asset Revenue (other	Dr. ↑ Cr. ↑	Interest Receivable 5 Interest Earned 5
	Bought $200 of merchandise on credit	Merchandise Accounts Payable	Cost of Goods Liability	Dr. ↑ Cr. ↑	Merchandise 200 Accounts Payable 200
	Sold merchandise on credit for $800 with a cost of $600	Accounts Receivable Cost of Goods Sold Sales Mer. Inventory	Asset Cost of Goods Sold Revenue Asset	Dr. ↑ Dr. ↑ Cr. → Cr. →	Accounts Receivable 800 Cost of Goods Sold 600 Sales 800 Merchandise 600
Depreciation	Discarded a fully depreciated machine—$2,000	Accum. Dep.—Mach. Machinery	Contra Asset Asset	Dr. → Cr. →	Accum. Deprec.—Mach. 2,000 Machinery 2,000
	Sold office equipment for $400 having cost of $750 and acc. dep. of $300	Cash Loss of sales-equip. Accum. Dep. Of. Eq. Office Equipment	Asset Owner's Equity Contra Asset Asset	Dr. ↑ Dr. ↑ Dr. → Cr. →	Cash 400 Loss of Sales—Equip. 50 Acc. Dep.—Equip. 300 Office Equipment 750
	Sold Office Equipment for $600 having a cost of $750 and acc. dep. of $300	Cash Acc. Dep.—Equip. Office Equipment Gain on sales—equip.	Asset Contra Asset Asset Revenue (other inc.)	Dr. ↑ Dr. → Cr. → Cr. ↑	Cash 600 Accum. Dep.—Equip. 300 Office Equipment 750 Gain on Sale of Equip. 150
	Exchanged old equipment and cash for new equipment— cost of old 1,800 acc. dep. 1,500 cost of new 1,950	Equipment Acc. Dep. Equip. Equipment Cash	Asset Contra Asset Asset Asset	Dr. ↑ Dr. → Cr. → Cr. →	Equipment (new) 1,950 Acc. Dep. Equip. 1,500 Equipment (old 1,850 Cash 1,650
Payroll	Recorded weekly payroll: Salaries $ 19.90 FICA 32.00 Medical 14.50 Union 11.50 Net Pay 320.10	Salary Expense FICA Payable FWT Payable Medical Payable Union Dues Payable Salaries Payable	Expense Liability Liability Liability Liability Liability	Dr. ↑ Cr. ↑ Cr. ↑ Cr. ↑ Cr. ↑ Cr. ↑	Salary Expense 398 FICA Payable 19.90 FWT Payable 32 Medical Payable 14.50 Union Payable 11.50 Salaries Payable 320.10
	Recorded employers taxes: FICA 19.90 State Unemployment 5.50 Federal Unemployment 2.50	Payroll Tax Expense FICA Tax Payable State Unempl. Tax Federal Unemp. Tax	Expense Liability Liability Liability	Dr. ↑ Cr. ↑ Cr. ↑ Cr. ↑	Payroll Tax Expense 27.90 FICA Tax Payable 19.90 State Unempl. Tax Pay. 5.50 Federal Un. Tax Payable 2.50

Area of Coverage in Text	The Situation	Typical Accounts Affected	Category	Rules	Sample Journal Entry That Would Result
	Employer makes monthly deposit: FICA (ee) 19.90 / FICA (er) 19.90 / FWT 32.00	FICA Payable / FWT Payable / Cash	Liability / Liability / Asset	Dr. / Dr. / Cr.	FICA Payable 39.80 / FWT Payable 32 / Cash 71.80
	Employer completes deposit for Federal Unemployment Deposit —$125	Federal Un. Tax / Cash	Liability / Asset	Dr. / Cr.	Federal Un. Tax Payable 125 / Cash 125
Corporations	Sold and issued 200 shares of $100 par value stock	Cash / Common Stock	Asset / Stockholder's Equity	Dr. / Cr.	Cash 20,000 / Common Stock 20,000
	A/ Received subscription to 5,000 shares of $5 par common stock at $6 per share / B/ With down payment of 50% of subscription price	Com. St. Sub. Rec. / Com. St. Subscribed / Prem. Comm. Stock / Cash / Comm. St. Sub. Rec.	Asset / Stockholder's Equity / Stockholder's Equity / Asset / Asset	Dr. / Cr. / Cr. / Dr. / Cr.	Com. St. Sub. Rec. 30,000 / Com. St. Subscribed 25,000 / Premium Com. Stock 5,000 / Cash 15,000 / Com. St. Sub. Rec. 15,000
	Received balance owed from subscribers and issued 5,000 shares of stock	A/ Cash / Com. St. Sub. Rec. / B/ Com. St. Sub. / Common Stock	Asset / Stockholder's Equity / Stockholder's Equity / Stockholder's Equity	Dr. / Cr. / Dr. / Cr.	Cash 15,000 / Com. St. Sub. Rec. 15,000 / Com. St. Subscribed 25,000 / Common Stock 25,000
	Directors declared a $2 per share dividend on the 10,000 shares of stock outstanding	Retained Earnings / Dividend Payable	Stockholder's Equity / Liability	Dr. / Cr.	Retained Earnings 20,000 / Dividend Payable 20,000
	Dividend previously declared is now paid	Dividend Payable / Cash	Liability / Asset	Dr. / Cr.	Dividend Payable 20,000 / Cash 20,000
	Sold 1,000 shares of $10 par common stock at $12 per share	Cash / Common Stock / Premium Com. Stock	Asset / Stockholder's Equity / Stockholder's Equity	Dr. / Cr. / Cr.	Cash 12,000 / Common Stock 10,000 / Premium Com. Stock 2,000

Area of Coverage in Text	The Situation	Typical Accounts Affected	Category	Rules	Sample Journal Entry That Would Result
	Sold 1,000 shares of $10 par common stock at $8 per share	Cash Dis. on Com. Stock Common Stock	Asset Stockholder's Equity Stockholder's Equity	↑ Dr. ↑ Dr. ↑ Cr.	Cash 8,000 Dis. on Common St. 2,000 Common Stock 10,000
	Purchased 200 shares of treasury stock at $120 per share (par is $100)	Treasury Stock Cash	Stockholder's Equity Asset	→ Dr. → Cr.	Treasury Stock 24,000 Cash 24,000

	Sold 100 shares of treasury stock at $150 that cost $120 per share	Cash
		Treasury Stock
		Contributed Capital
			Asset
			Stockholder's Equity
			Stockholder's Equity
				↑ Dr.
				↑ Cr.
				↑ Cr.
					Cash 15,000
					   Treasury Stock 12,000
					   Contributed Capital 3,000

	Sold 100 shares of treasury stock at $110 that cost $120 per share	Cash Contributed Capital Treasury Stock	Asset Stockholder's Equity Stockholder's Equity	↑ Dr. → Dr. ↑ Cr.	Cash 11,000 Contributed Capital 1,000 Treasury Stock 12,000

	Declared a stock dividend (1,000 shares) on $25 par stock. Current market value is $50	Retained Earnings
		Common Stock Distri.
		Premium Com. Stock
			Stockholder's Equity
			Stockholder's Equity
			Stockholder's Equity
				→ Dr.
				↑ Cr.
				↑ Cr.
					Retained Earnings 50,000
					   Com. Stock Div. Dist. 25,000
					   Prem. on Com. Stock 25,000

	Recorded the distribution of the stock dividend	Common St. Div. Common Stock	Stockholder's Equity Stockholder's Equity	→ Dr. ↑ Cr.	Comm. Stock Di. Dist. 25,000 Common Stock 25,000
Bonds	Sold $2,000,000 of bonds at a discount for $1,950,000	Cash Dis. on Bonds Pay. Bonds Payable	Asset Liability Liability	↑ Dr. ↑ Dr. ↑ Cr.	Cash 1,950,000 Dis. on Bonds Pay. 50,000 Bonds Payable 2,000,000

	Sold 2,000,000 of bonds at a premium of $2,050,000	Cash
		Premium Bonds Pay.
		Bonds Payable
			Asset
			Liability
			Liability
				↑ Dr.
				↑ Cr.
				↑ Cr.
					Cash 2,050,000
					   Prem. Bonds Pay. 50,000
					   Bonds Payable 2,000,000

Area of Coverage in Text	The Situation	Typical Accounts Affected	Category	Rules	Sample Journal Entry That Would Result
	Paid semi-annual interest on the bonds $15,000	Interest Expense Cash	Expense Asset	Dr. ↑ Cr. →	Interest Expense 15,000 Cash 15,000
	Accrued interest on bonds $5,000	Interest Expense Interest Payable	Expense Liability	Dr. ↑ Cr. ←	Interest Expense 5,000 Interest Payable 5,000
	Paid interest expense of $3,000 and amortized $250 of the bond premium	Bond Interest Exp. Premium Bonds Pay. Cash	Expense Stockholder's Equity Asset	Dr. ↑ Dr. → Cr. →	Bonds Interest Expense 3,000 Premium Bonds Payable 250 Cash 3,250
	Deposited $5,000 with sinking fund trustee	Bond Sinking Fund Cash	Long-Term Invest. (asset) Asset	Dr. ↑ Cr. →	Bond Sinking Fund 5,000 Cash 5,000
	Paid Bonds $100,000 and returned additional cash from sinking fund of $2,000	Cash Bonds Payable Bond Sink. Fund	Asset Liability Long-Term Invest.	Dr. ↑ Dr. → Cr. →	Cash 2,000 Bonds Payable 100,000 Bonds Sinking Fund 102,000

Appendix III Key Managerial and Cost Terms

Absorption costing: A product costing method of measuring earnings on the Income Statement in which all manufacturing costs (fixed and variable) are treated as product costs to the units produced.

Accretion: Increase in economic worth by natural development. Example includes timber orchards, etc.

Acid test: A financial ratio that measures a companies current debt-paying ability.

Asset turnover: A financial ratio which shows sales divided by total assets.

Average age of receivables: Accounts Receivable of company divided by yearly sales times 365.

Break even analysis: That level of business operations for a company where total costs equal total revenue.

Budget: A formal financial plan of action.

By product: A joint product that has little sales value in comparison to the products produced in the process. The costs that are assigned to these by products reduce costs of the primary products. Example: wood shavings.

Capital budgeting: A firms long-range investment in plant and equipment.

Consolidated financial statements: Financial statements that show the firms financial position and income if they were one single economic entity although they are legally separate companies.

Contribution margin: The excess of revenue (sales) over a firms variable costs. The difference aids in absorbing fixed costs.

Example: Product Cost 40.00
    variable cost <u>25.00</u>
  Contri. margin 15.00

Differential cost: The difference in a firms cost resulting from a change in levels of production.

Direct costs: The firms cost of direct materials, overhead that results in producing a particular product.

Direct labor: The cost of labor that works *directly* on materials in the manufacturing process.

Equivalent units: Used in process costing to calculate how the dollar of costs are allocated between the finished goods and the goods in process. Ex. a unit 60% complete has only 60% of the labor cost charged to it as compared to a finished good of 100%.

Factory overhead: All manufacturing costs other than direct labor or direct materials.

Finished goods: Units of a product that for which manufacturing has been completed, but finished goods is a current asset on the balance sheet.

Fixed cost: Any cost whose total remains constant as the activity of the operations of the company changes.

Indirect cost: Cost which are not easily identified as certain department and thus the cost is spread among departments.

Inventory turnover: The financial statement ratio that shows cost of goods sold divided by average inventory.

Job cost card (sheets): Basically the work in process account's subsidiary ledger.

Job order cost-accounting: Manufacturing costs are assigned to each job(s) in a perpetual inventory system.

Marginal cost: The additional cost associated with producing one more unit of a product.

Overapplied overhead: The situation where more overhead was transferred to work in process than estimated. The balance of the account is a credit.

Process cost accounting: A perpetual inventory accounting system that accumulates costs according to specific departments process in the firm.

Raw materials inventory: Those goods used in the manufacturing of a product. These goods, classified as an asset, on the balance sheet.

Standard cost: The anticipated cost that should have been incurred in producing a unit of output.

Sunk cost: Cost incurred in the past which cannot be changed by current decision facing the firm.

Underapplied overhead: The situation where less overhead was transferred to work in process than estimated. The balance of an account is a debit.

Variable cost: Cost which responds directly as the level of the firms operations increase or decrease.

Variable costing: The procedure in product costing in which only variable manufacturing costs are identified with a product. The fixed costs are treated as end of period costs.

Variances: Difference that arises (favorable, or unfavorable) between standard and actual costs.

Index

Accelerated depreciation—see declining balance—sum-of-years, 78, 200
Account, 3
Account number—see post reference, 157
Accounting, 3
Accounting cycle, 4
Accounting equation, 5
Accounting period, 6
Accounting principles, 6
Accounts payable, 7
Accounts payable ledger (subsidiary ledger), 7
Accounts receivable, 8
Accounts receivable ledger (subsidiary ledger), 8
Accrual basis of accounting, 9
Accrued expenses, 10-11
Accrued interest expense, 12-13
Accrued payables—see accrued expenses, 10-11
Accrued revenue, 13
Accumulated depreciation, 14-15
Adjusted trial balance, 16-17
Adjusting entries, 18-19
After-closing balance—see post-closing trial balance, 156
Aging accounts receivable, 20
Allowance for doubtful accounts—see contra accounts, 61
Allowance method for bad debts, 21-22
Amortization, 23
Analysis of trade receivables—see aging accounts receivable, 20
Appropriation of retained earnings, 24
Assets, 25
Auditing, 25
Average cost—see weighted average of inventory costing, 215

Bad debts, 26
Balance column account, 26
Balance sheet (position statement), 27

Balance sheet expenditure—see capital expenditure, 41
Balancing and ruling, 28
Bank discount, 28
Bank loan, 29
Bank reconciliation, 30-31
Bearer bonds—see coupon bonds, 67
Beginning inventory—merchandise company, 32
Betterment, 33
Bill—see invoice, 119
Bond, 33
Bond discount, 34
Bond—face value, 35
Bond payable—see bound discount, 34
Bond premium, 36
Book of original entry—see journal, 120
Book value—equipment, 37
Book value—equity per share of stock, 38
Bookkeeping, 39
Business entity, 39
Business transaction—see invoice, 119

Calendar year, 40
Callable bonds, 40
Capital (owners' equity, net worth), 41
Capital expenditure, 41
Capital statement, 42
Capital stock—see common stock, 56
Cash basis of accounting, 43
Cash disbursements journal (cash payments journal), 46-47
Cash discount, 44
Cash dividend, 45
Cash—flow statement, 50
Cash receipts journal, 48-49
Certified public accountant (CPA), 51
Changes in financial position statement—see funds statement, 104
Charge—see on account, 143
Chart of accounts, 51

Check register, 52
Checks in transit—see outstanding checks, 145
Classified balance sheet (position statement), 52-53
Classified position statement—see classified balance sheet, 52-53
Clearing entries—see closing entries, 55
Closed accounts—see closing entries, 55
Closing entries, 55
Common-size statements, 54
Common stock, 56
Comparative statements, 57
Compound journal entry, 58
Computer, 58
Computer program, 59
Conservatism—see principle of conservatism, 162
Consistency—see principles of consistency, 162
Contingent liability—notes receivable, 60
Contra asset—see contra account, 61
Contra account—accumulated depreciation, allowance for doubtful accounts, 61
Contributed capital—see paid-in capital, 196
Contribution margin—see departmental margin, 82
Controlling account—accounts payable, 62
Controlling account—accounts receivable, 63
Convertible bond, 64
Corporation, 64
Cost of goods sold (cost of sales)—merchandising company, 65
Cost or market, 66
Cost principle, 66
Coupon bonds (bearer bonds), 67
CPA—See Certified public accountant, 51
Credit (debit, credit), 67
Credit memorandum, 68-69
Creditors, 70
Cross-reference—see post-reference, 156
Crossword accounting review puzzles
Accounts I, II mix, 238, 239, 240
Accounting hunt, 241, 242
Accrual and deferrals, 226, 227
Adjusting and closing entries, 222, 223

Corporations, 232-333
Depreciation, 228, 229
Journals, 224, 225
Merchandise company (cost of goods sold), 234, 235
Notes and interest, 230-231
Rules of debits and credits, 220, 221
Voucher system, 236, 237
Solutions to puzzles, 243-245
Cumulative preferred stock, 70
Current assets, 71
Current liabilities, 72
Current ratio, 72

Data processing—see computer, 58
Date of declaration, 73
Date of payment, 74
Date of record, 74
Days in a month rule, 75
Debenture bonds, 76
Debit (debits, credits), 76
Debit memorandum, 77
Declining-balance method of depreciation, 78
Defaulting—notes receivable, 79
Deferral, 80
Deferred charges—see prepaid expenses, 161
Deferred revenue—see unearned revenue, 207-8
Deficit—retained earnings, 81
Departmental margin (contribution margin), 82
Depletion, 83
Deposit in transit—see bank reconciliation, 30-31
Depreciation, 83
Direct charge-off method—see direct write-off method for bad debts, 85
Direct labor—manufacturing business, 84
Direct materials—manufacturing business, 84
Direct write-off method for bad debts, 85
Disclosure—see principle of consistency, 162
Discount on stock, 86
Discounted notes receivable, 87
Dishonored notes receivable, 88
Dividend, 88
Dividend in arrears, 89
Double declining—see declining balance, 78

Double-entry bookkeeping, 90
Drawings—see withdrawal, 216

Earned surplus—see retained earnings, 177
Earnings per share, 91
Earnings statement—see income statement, 115
Employee, 91
Employees earning record, 92
Employer, 92
Employer's payroll taxes, 93
Ending inventory—merchandise company, 94
Equity, 95
Equity per share—see book value—equity per share of stock, 38
Estimated uncollectibles—see contra account, 61
Expense and revenue summary—see income summary, 116
Expenses, 95
Expired costs, 96
Extraordinary items, 96

Factory overhead—manufacturing business, 97
Federal Insurance Contribution Act—see FICA, 97
Federal unemployment conpensation—see employer's payroll taxes, 93

FICA, 97
Financial statements—see balance sheet, income statement, 115
Finished goods account—manufacturing company, 98
FIFO—see first-in, first-out, 99
First-in, first-out (FIFO), 99
Fiscal year (natural business year), 100
Fixed assets (plant assets, tangible assets, noncurrent assets), 100
Fixed liabilities, 101
FOB destination (free on board), 101
FOB shipping point (free on board), 102
Folio—see post-reference, 157
Footing—see pencil footing, 152
Freight-in, 103
Fund statement (change in financial position), 104
Funds, 105
Funds-flow statement—see change in financial position, 104

General journal, 105-106
General ledger (principle ledger), 107
Going concern, 108
Goods available for sale—see cost of goods sold, 65
Goods in process—see work in process, 215
Goodwill, 109
Gross margin—see gross profit, 110-111
Gross pay, 109
Gross profit (gross margin), 110-111
Gross profit method, 112
Gross sales, 113

Horizontal analysis of statements, 114

Income statement (earnings statement, operating statement), 115
Income summary (expense and revenue summary account), 116
Intangible assets, 117
Interest, 117
Interest calculations—see six percent, sixty-day method, 189
Interim statements, 118
Internal control, 118-119
Internal transaction—see depreciation, 83
Inventory—see periodic or perpetual, 152-153
Invoice, 119

Journal, 120
Journal entry, 120
Journalizing transactions, 121

Last-in, first-out (LIFO), 122
Ledger, 123
Legal capital—see minimum legal capital, 133
Liabilities (creditors), 124
LIFO—see last-in, first-out, 122
Limited liability, 125
Liquid assets (quick assets), 125
Liquidation (partnership), 126-127
Long-term assets—see long-term investment, 128
Long-term investments, 128
Long-term liabilities, 129
Lower of cost or market—see cost or market, 66

Maker, 130
Market rate for bond interest—see bond premium or bond discount, 34, 36

Market value per share—see stock split, 195
Marketable securities, 130
Matching principle, 131
Materiality—see principle of materiality, 163
Maturity date, 131
Merchandise company, 132
Merchandise inventory—merchandise company, 132
Minimum legal capital, 133

Miscellaneous account—see sundry account, 200
Mortgage notes payable, 134

Natural business year—see fiscal year, 100
Negative account—see contra account, 61
Negotiable instrument, 135
Net income (net profit), 135
Net loss, 136
Net pay, 137
Net purchases—see cost of goods sold, 65
Net profit—see net income, 135
Net realizable value—see contra account, 61
Net sales, 138
Net worth—see capital, 41
Nominal accounts (temporary accounts), 139
Noncumulative preferred stock, 140
Noncurrent assets—see fixed assets, 100
Nonparticipating preferred stock, 140-141
Normal balance account, 142
Notes payable, 142
Notes receivable, 143

Objective evidence—see principle of objectivity, 163
On account, 143
Operating statement—see income statement, 115
Organization costs, 144
Output method—see units of production, 208
Outstanding checks (checks in transit), 145
Owner's equity—see capital, 41

Paid-in capital (contributed capital), 196

Parent company—see subsidiary company, 199
Par value, 146
Participating preferred stock, 147
Partnership, 148
Patents (intangible asset), 148
Payable, 149
Payee—promissory note, 149
Payroll, 150
Payroll register, 151
Pencil footing, 152
Periodic inventory system, 152-153
Permanent accounts—see real accounts, 172
Perpetual inventory system, 153-4
Petty cash fund, 155
Plant asset—see fixed asset, 100
Position statement—see balance sheet, 27
Post-clearing trial balance—see post-closing trial balance, 156
Post-closing trial balance (post-clearing trial balance), 156
Posting rules—see individual journals (cash disbursements, cash receipts, sales, purchases)
Posting—see post-reference, 157
Post-reference (folio), 157
Principle ledger—see general ledger, 107
Preemptive right, 158
Preferred stock, 159
Premium on stock, 160
Prepaid expenses, 161
Prepaid rent, 161
Principal—see maturity date, 131
Principle of conservatism, 162
Principle of consistency, 162
Principle of materiality, 163
Principle of objectivity, 163
Private accountant, 164
Proceeds—see discounted notes receivable, 87
Profit and loss summary—see income summary, 116
Proprietorship—see sold proprietorship, 190
Promissory note, 164
Protest notice, 165
Public accountant, 165
Punch card, 166
Purchase account, 166
Purchase discount account, 167
Purchase journal, 168
Purchase order, 169

268

Purchase returns and allowance account, 170

Quick assets (liquid assets), 170

Rate of return on assets, 171
Rate of return on equity (stockholders), 172
Raw material inventory—see work in process, 216
Real accounts (permanent), 172
Realization—partnership, 173-4
Recording transactions—see journalizing transactions, 121
Redemption—see callable bonds, 40
Registered bonds, 174
Residual value, 175
Retail method—inventory, 176
Retained earnings, 177
Retained earnings statement, 177
Revenue, 178
Revenue expenditure, 178
Reversing entry, 179-180
Rules of debits and credits, 181

Salaries payable, 181
Sales discount, 182
Sales journal, 183
Sales return and allowance account, 183-4
Salvage value, 184
Schedule of accounts payable, 185
Schedule of accounts receivable, 186
Scrap value, 187
Secured bonds, 187
Securities—see marketable securities, 130
Serial bonds, 188
Shareholders—see stockholders, 196
Shareholders equity—see stockholders equity, 196
Shareholders liability—see limited liability, 125
Sinking fund bonds, 188
Six percent, sixty-day method, 189
Sixty-day, six percent method, 189
Slide, 189
Sole proprietorship, 190
Sources of funds—see fund statement, 105
Special journal, 190
State unemployment compensation tax—see employer's payroll taxes, 93

Stated value of stock, 191
Statement analysis, 192
Stock, 192
Stock certificate, 193
Stock dividend, 194
Stock split (stock split-up), 195
Stockholders (shareholders), 196
Stockholders equity (shareholders equity), 196
Stockholders liability—see limited liability, 125
Straight-line method of depreciation, 197
Subscriptions (receivable), 198
Subsidiary company, 199
Subsidiary ledger—see accounts payable ledger, 7
Subsidiary ledger—see accounts receivable ledger, 8
Sum-of-the-year's digit method of depreciation, 200
Sundry account column (miscellaneous account), 200

T-account, 201
Tangible asset—see fixed asset, 100
Temporary account—see nominal account, 139
Temporary investments—see marketable securities, 130
Term bonds, 201
Terms—see cash discount, 44
Trade discounts, 202
Trade-in value, 203
Transactions, 203
Transportation-in—see freight-in, 103
Transportation terms—see FOB destination or FOB shipping point, 102-103
Transportation, 204
Treasury stock, 204
Trial balance, 205

Unadjusted trial balance, 206
Uncollectable account—see direct write-off or allowance method, 85, 21-22
Underwriter, 207
Unearned revenue, 207-8
Units-of-production (output method of depreciation), 208
Unlimited liability, 209
Uses of funds—see fund statement, 104

Vertical analysis of statements, 210
Voucher, 211
Voucher payable, 211
Voucher register, 212
Voucher system, 213

W-2, 213
W-4, 213
Wages payable—see salaries payable, 190

Wage and tax statement—see W-2, 213
Weighted average of inventory costing, 215
Withdrawal, 216
Withholding exemption certificate—see W-4, 214
Work in process account—manufacturing company, 216
Working capital, 217
Work sheet, 217, 218

NOTES

NOTES

NOTES